To Algre Gregory
from The author
John O'Dwyer

Desmond Cleagh.

A GLOSSARY OF
ART TERMS

A GLOSSARY OF ART TERMS

by

John O'Dwyer *and* Raymond Le Mage

with a foreword by
Ruskin Spear A.R.A.

PETER NEVILL LIMITED

London *New York*

PETER NEVILL LIMITED
50 Old Brompton Road
London SW7 and 122
East 55th Street New York 22

Made and printed in Great Britain by John R Lawes and
Co Ltd 31 Brighton Road South Croydon Surrey

MCML

FOREWORD

On a warm summer day, and after a heavier lunch than usual, W. G. Grace was reluctant to spend an afternoon in the field. The two captains tossed for first innings. "Donkey" roared Grace, and as the coin dropped "Donkey it is!" The young captain of the public school eleven would not bring himself to confess his ignorance of whether 'Donkey' stood for tail or head. Grace went in to bat.

I should not like to suggest that the professional writer on art, in his relationship to the reader, is in an analagous position to Grace in that story. But the present position becomes increasingly one of a closed circle of artists and critics talking an obscure language to the confusion of even the most intelligent layman.

It may not be important to most of us to know what Dadaism was or what the Nabis believed in — it may be as irrelevant to us now as a dictionary definition of John Ruskin's 'Pot of Paint' in the famous Whistler episode. But should anyone want to know the answers are here together with a great deal of information of a similar nature. This Glossary of Art Terms is, in fact, full of interesting and carefully documented knowledge and is in parts almost a text book on painting. Both Mr. O'Dwyer and Mr. Le Mage are to be warmly congratulated for their enthusiasm. A book of this kind has been needed for some time.

RUSKIN SPEAR A.R.A.

PREFACE

In compiling this glossary the authors had in mind the needs of the large public with a newly-awakened intelligent interest in art which has sprung into being since the war. The language of art bristles with esoteric words and references, and anyone whose interest in painting or sculpture is aroused, perhaps for the first time, by a visit to an exhibition is bound to be perplexed and discouraged by the numerous unfamiliar terms and references to schools, groups and movements that he finds in his catalogue notes, or later, if he pursues his interest, in the columns of art criticism in newspapers and periodicals and in broadcast talks. This applies particularly to modern art where a subtle language has been evolved by a race of artists and critics far more intellectual than their predecessors, and where the history is so recent and complex.

The authors have therefore placed emphasis on modern art, its language, schools and movements, and have selected the terms to be defined largely on the basis of the frequency with which they recur in current art criticism. It is, of course, impossible to be in any way comprehensive in so short a work, and we do not expect to meet the needs of the experienced art student, but the average person with a keen but untutored interest in art will, we believe, find here the answers to most of those teasing little queries which arise when reading his favourite art critic in the week-end papers.

John O'Dwyer

Raymond Le Mage

" . . . . . . on the effort to understand art depends the effort to understand life, to understand the principle of liberty which makes life, and which makes human progress."

HERBERT READ

A

Abbozzio (It.)   The sketch or preliminary draft of a work of art.

Abstract Art   Abstraction in art may be best defined as the representation of forms devoid of emotional associations or imitative intention. Ideally, abstract art is *form* without *content*. An artist may find the theme for an abstract picture either in the material world or in the invention, of imaginary forms, but in either case the abstractionist is concerned solely with producing a composition of line and colour aesthetically pleasing in itself. Pure abstract art is the exact opposite of *Naturalism.* (q.v.).

Mr. Jan Gordon has said "complete abstractionists are somehow rather dull" — a fact which a good many artists would seem to have realised in that most " abstract " paintings can be more accurately described as *near-abstract* (where the design is derived from natural forms) or even *semi abstract* (where the natural forms are much more strongly suggested).

The idea of abstraction was first systematically explored by the Cubists (See CUBISM) in the early part of the present century in revolt against the naturalist tradition which had culminated in the Impressionist movement, and was adopted and modified to suit the requirements of various groups of artists. In the hands of Ozenfant and Le Corbusier it became known as *Purism* (q.v.) and it was a strong influence upon *Synchromism, Orphism, Futurism, Dadaism, Surrealism* and *Expressionism* (qq.v.). It was applied to photography and the film by Man Ray, Moholy-Nagy, Léger and Richter, and it became completely abstract and geometric with the Dutch *"De Stijl"* group and *Neo-Plasticism* (qq.v.) ; with the Russian *Suprematism* and *Constructivism* (qq.v.); with the French group

Abstraction-Création and the English abstractionists, Wadsworth and Nicholson.

Abstraction-Création   A group of geometric-abstract painters and sculptors in Paris in the early 1930's, led by Piet Mondriaan and Jean Hélion.

Academicism is the conservative element in art which sanctions over a period of time the artistic heresies of to-day. In this country a large proportion of the paintings accepted by "art lovers" are Impressionist in inspiration.

Académie Suisse   An informal art school in Paris in the 1860's where there was no tuition but always a model, and where the artists dropped in to draw from the figure as they pleased.

Academy Figure   A study of the human figure posed to display the action of the muscles. Also, any figure in a conventional pose which is designed to display the artist's skill in composition. A figure in a picture is of academic proportions when it is little under half natural size.

Accidentals   In painting, those effects of light not accounted for by the main source of illumination, e.g. firelight in an otherwise lighted room. Also, any qualities which, essential though they may be to the finish of a picture, are incidental to the basic conception of the artist. In the theory of abstract art, the artist regards as *accidental* the commonly accepted appearance of an object as opposed to his perception of its universal form. (See UNIVERSALS).

Acroliths   Archaic Greek statues in which the bodies were made of wood, while the head, hands and feet were of marble or stone. The bodies were sometimes clothed, gilded or overlaid with gold.

Acroteria   Marble or terra-cotta ornaments which crowned the pediments of Greek temples.

Action The representation of the movement of figures or objects within a painting. (See MOVEMENT).

Ada Group, School of the School of Carolingian miniature painters localised in the lower Rhineland, named after the Abbess Ada of Mainz who, about the year 800, commissioned a famous *evangeliar* (q.v.).

Aegean Vases were those produced by the Cretan civilization. Those of the early Minoan period (3400-2100 B.C.) were small and of egg-shell delicacy, while those of the middle Minoan period (2100-1580 B.C.) were graceful copies of metal vases decorated with geometric and formalized floral patterns and were known as Kamares ware. The finest Cretan ware was produced by the late Minoan period (1880-1200 B.C.). These at first were finely shaped vases decorated with naturalistic marine and floral patterns and were followed by the dignified Palace Style in which naturalistic design gave way to a formal pattern. The pottery produced at the end of this period was a very inferior ware crudely decorated with geometric patterns.

Aerial Perspective The representation of distance in a painting based upon the fact that because of the intervening atmosphere objects tend to lose their edges the more they recede into the background, darks are modified towards a uniform pale blue-grey, while lights are either left unchanged or appear warmer. The term Aerial Perspective would seem to be more precisely applied to the scientific principles underlying this theory, whereas in discussing the methods used to render this effect the terms *Atmospheric Perspective* and *Colour Perspective* seem to be more commonly used.

Aesthetic Emotion The pleasurable sensation that results from the contemplation of a work of art and, according to Mr. Clive Bell, the test of the value of a work of art. Such a personal and intimate reaction is not readily definable, although Mr. Bell describes it as "a passionate emotion", an "intense rapture," a "superhuman ecstacy" which transports the spectator to "superb peaks of aesthetic exaltation," while Mr. Hilaire Hiler has defined it as a pain in the solar plexus akin to that experienced when suddenly going down in a lift.

Aesthetic Movement A movement during the eighties of the last century which carried the ideal of beauty and the doctrine of art for art's sake to extravagant lengths accompanied by affectation of speech and manner and eccentricity of dress. Oscar Wilde was the chief apostle of this cult, and this aspect of Wilde has been perfectly burlesqued in the character of Bunthorne in Gilbert and Sullivan's comic opera *Patience*.

Aesthetics The term applied to that branch of philosophy which treats of artistic creation and appreciation, derived from the Greek word *aistheta* which means objects of sensuous as opposed to intellectual knowledge. The purpose of aesthetics is the discovery and formulation of universal laws of art and the establishment of a criterion for assessing the merit of a work of art.

Agalma Greek term for an article of sculpture, and occasionally applied to a painting, particularly a portrait.

Akkhr The initials of the Artists' Association of Revolutionary Russia, the largest group of the school of naturalistic representation, which arose in Russia in 1927 as a reaction against the abstract and expressionist tendencies in art. The Association was government sponsored and encouraged the production of pictures illustrating the revolution mainly for propaganda purposes.

Alla Prima (It.) The completion of a painting by a single application of all the pigments as opposed to their application in successive layers at various intervals.

4

Altarpiece   A series of fixed or movable panels, usually painted or sculpted in relief, placed at the back of an altar.

Altogether, The   Studio euphemism for posing in the nude.

Alto-Relievo (It.)   Sculpture in high relief.

Amalaka (Sanskrit)   The bulbous form surmounting the towers of Indian Temples.

American Aboriginal Art   With the exception of certain archaic Mayan sculptures and some gigantic statuary in eastern Columbia (and possibly the gold and bronze casting of the Chibchas and Quimbayas in ancient Columbia which, although technically perfect, retains the characteristics of really primitive art), the arts of Mexico and Central America (i.e. the Aztecs, Mayas and Incas) are products of too highly developed a civilization to be properly dealt with under this heading.

A truly aboriginal art, however, is found among the North American Indians.   In fact, the centres of their culture on the north west coast and islands form one of the most important districts of primitive art in the world.   Theirs was essentially an heraldic art based upon Totemic beliefs and a vast store of legend.   The style was normally highly conventional as in their monumental Totem poles, large wall paintings and Chilkat blankets with their mysterious "eye ornaments", but there is also evidence of a more naturalistic style in the earlier rock engravings at Nanaimo, Vancouver Island.   And there is a highly realistic sculpture in the modern portrait statues of the Haida Indians of British Columbia.

Other forms of truly primitive art are to be found in the polychrome paintings on buffalo hide of the Plains Indians (the purely geometric patterns were the work of women while representative forms were painted by the men), the paintings and pottery of the Pueblo Indians of New Mexico and Arizona, the stone carving of the "moundbuilders" in the Eastern States and Texas and in the wooden masks of the modern Iroquois.

The art of the Eskimos is characterised by their graphic art which takes the form of highly realistic engravings of Eskimo life on ivory.

American Art   It may be easily understood that the art of the early American Colonies depended on the immigration of European artists who, in the circumstances, would hardly be of the first order. It is not until the advent of Benjamin West (1738-1820) that we find the beginning of a truly national art which still depended on European traditions as, in the main, it continued to do until recent years.   Winslow Homer (1836 - 1910) is generally acknowledged to be the most American in his art, his seascapes being distinguished for their vigour and character.   (See ASHCAN SCHOOL, BARBIZON SCHOOL, DIRECT PAINTING, HUDSON RIVER SCHOOL, LUMINISTS, TONALISM).

The broadly realistic American tradition is being challenged to-day by the growth of a new school of non-representational painting influenced by Post-Impressionist trends from Paris which has gained impetus from the actual arrival of a host of continental artist refugees including Léger, Masson, Ernst, Tanguy and Mondriaan.   There has not, however, been any wholesale acceptance of continental "isms," rather has there been a selecting and crossing of styles from which emerge several distinct native types resulting in the evolution of a dynamic American picture.   Typical of this development is the work of Feininger, Dove, Marin, Xcéron, Bauer and Stuart Davis, the best known of the American Abstractionists.   The younger artists (e.g. John Seenhauser, Seymour Franks and Oscar Fischinger) have managed to convey the pace and tempo of American life with a style derived from the air view and the air map, and that the film has had its sphere of influence is evidenced by such devices as the multiple or split image. Steve Wheeler is perhaps the best known of the group which has drawn inspiration from American Indian motifs, and Ellwood Graham and Adolf Gottlied are developing a new symbolism through their exploration of the Indian pictograph. (See also SYNCHROMISM and "291").

Amorino (It.)   A cupid, common in Italian 16th cent. sculpture and painting.

Antwerp School   A school of painting which succeeded the School of Bruges as the centre of Flemish art between the years 1480-1505, and which included principally the painters Massys, Mabuse, Patinir, Bles, Pieter Brueghel, Snyders and Seghers.

Apotropaic Eye   In Greek art the representation of the human eye on objects (e.g. ships) to ward off evil.

Applied Art   Those arts which are concerned with the production of useful objects as distinct from works of purely aesthetic significance. The distinction, which is roughly the difference between the products of the craftsman and the artist, is often difficult to make.   Compare, for example, a piece of modern table ware and an article of Sung ware.   Both are products of the potter; but whereas the former, while possessing artistic merit, is merely functional in intention, the latter is almost entirely the product of a highly developed artistic consciousness.

Appliqué   A design or pattern formed in outline in one material and laid upon another.   Used in various crafts, particularly needlework and metalwork.

Aquarelle   A drawing (either original or a print) coloured with transparent watercolour washes.

Aquatint   A method of engraving which like *etching* (q.v) involves the use of a mordant acid, but differs in that it is used to render tonal effects instead of lines. These tones graduate from rich deep passages to light transparent tints similar in effect to water-colour paintings, hence the name aqua, or water, tint. The process has been used, notably by Goya, to supplement the etched line with remarkably fine effect.

Arabesque Surface decoration in colour or low-relief composed of flowing lines and patterns of flowers, leaves, branches and scroll work fancifully inter-twined.

Archaic Greek Sculpture Sculpture produced in Greece during the 6th and early 5th cents. B.C. It is the work of masters of formalized design, who yet attempted to render the human figure with increasing naturalism, so that their sculpture, al-though based on severe geometric designs, is possessed of a certain charm and vitality. The best examples of their work are the votive statues of youths and maidens (kouri and kourai) which in their rigidity are reminiscent of Egyptian sculpture but which possess a greater humanistic element in their facial expressiveness.

Archaistic Sculpture A form of Graeco-Roman sculpture which, in reaction against the realistic sculpture of Hellenistic times, took as its model the simple and formal sculpture of Archaic Greece of the 6th cent. B.C.

Architectonic The structural or architectural element in a design or composition; the sense of formal order desirable in painting and sculpture; the perfect integration of line, form and colour in a work of art.

Architectural Art Term first employed by the critic R. H. Wilenski to describe the attitude of the classic artist as opposed to the romantic artist, in so far as the one, like the architect, conceives his work

8

as a succession of co-ordinated ideas which culminate in a highly formal composition, while the other permits it to evolve from an intense emotional experience arising from his contemplation of a particular object. (See EMOTIVE FRAGMENT).

Architecture   Apart from being the "Mother of the Arts" in the sense that most artistic activity was originally concerned with the embellishment of The Building, architecture has always been the archetype of the arts in so far as the concepts which lie behind architecture as an art (proportion, balance, line, recession, etc.) have always been the ideal concepts behind the great Classical tradition in painting and sculpture.   Exponents of the modern movement in painting and sculpture, with their classical preoccupation with formal relationships, regard the architect's problem as substantially their own.   They see in the well-designed building the successful expression of that formal order or architecture in the universe towards which their own art aspires.   One apologist of the modern movement has stated, "The idea of art on which the modern movement is based is the idea that the typical function of the architect as artist is the typical function of the painter and sculptor as well".

Armature (Sculp.)   Framework, usually of metal, used by the sculptor as a skeleton around which to mould the clay when modelling a figure.

Arriccio   In fresco painting the first, coarsest and thickest coat of plaster applied to the wall.

Art for Art's Sake   The much ridiculed slogan of the *Aesthetic Movement* (q.v.).

In a new preface addressed to artists in the 1945 edition of R. H. Wilenski's "The Modern Movement in Art," the author points out that anti-democratic propagandists are out to "destroy the artist's initiative" because art is concerned with "aspects of life beyond the range of authoritarian

9

control" so that thereafter they may exploit him "for the increase of their own power." In spite of the derision and contempt which still adheres to the phrase "Art for art's sake," it remains for the artist a far safer cry than "Art as Public Service" or "Art for the Party's Sake."

Artist   Although everyone knows what an artist is, the compilers of this glossary would like to contribute to precision in the use of this word by emphasising that the facile trick of producing a likeness of anything in paint or stone can be learned and developed to a high degree of accuracy by any apt student in two or three years. The fundamental and essential attributes of an artist, originality and imagination, cannot be learned.

Artistic Problem   An expression used to describe all those difficulties, technical and psychological, which beset the artist when he begins to interpret his original vision in the medium of his choice.

Art Nouveau (Fr. New Art)   The name given to a style in art which flourished between 1890 and 1905 in France, Belgium, Germany and to a lesser extent in England, Spain, Holland, Italy and the U.S.A. The movement aimed to break with the old traditions and create a new style with the use of the new materials, cement, iron, steel and glass, and the style was characterised by an excessive fluency of design and an unrestrained use of decoration on any available surface. Architecture, sculpture, painting and the graphic arts, furniture, wall paper, stained glass, metals, ceramics and jewelry were all influenced. Ironwork was tortured into every shape and form, furniture was shaped like animals, birds and insects, and cupboard doors and chairbacks were fretted with heart-shaped holes. Fantasy, in short, was allowed full play. The movement died of its own extravagance, and fashionable taste turned to more traditional forms.

Art of Free Fancy   This phrase describes the highly imaginative, uninhibited and often whimsical art form of which Paul Klee is the original exponent. The form has been described as "going for a walk with a line" and the line may take us anywhere according to the artist's fancy, usually into what has been described as an "intellectual fairyland". We can think of no better description of the art than Dr. Herbert Read's "the eye of the artist is concentrated on his pencil; the pencil moves and the line dreams."

Arts and Crafts Movement   The name given to the English revival of decorative art which began about 1875 as a revolt against the insularity of academic art and the extreme vulgarity of domestic design and furnishings. The movement crystallized in the Arts and Crafts Exhibition Society which held its first exhibition at the New Gallery in 1888. The revival was largely inspired by the work of William Morris, Rossetti and Burne-Jones in the realm of design and handicraft, by the work of Norman Shaw and Philip Webb in architecture and by that of William de Morgan in pottery.

Art Therapy   A recent branch of occupational therapy pioneered by Mr. Adrian Hill (See his "Art Versus Illness," Allen and Unwin, 1945) in which the practice of drawing and painting by convalescent patients, particularly in cases of slow recovery as in tuberculosis, is encouraged so as promote an active, purposeful and healthy state of mind.

Ashcan School, The (or, The Eight)   A term derisively applied to a Philadelphia group of American painters in 1908, George Luks, William Glackens, Robert Henri, Everett Shinn, John Sloane, Arthur B. Davies, M. Prendergast and E. Lawson, who sought to document objectively their immediate surroundings.

Associationism   This term was first applied to the theory, prevailing in the 1920's, that all art is one, that "a Persian bowl, Chinese carpets, Giotto's frescos and the masterpieces of Poussin, Piero della Francesca and Cézanne" all have a common quality as works of art.   Later, the term began to be used to describe the Surrealist method of associating seemingly incongruous articles and scenes in a composition, "chairs grouped together in the solitude of a Grecian plain with antique ruins", a tree in a room, a bedstead on the seashore.

Asymmetry   Balance is very often achieved in a design or composition without strict correspondence between the two sides of the work, an effect which usually produces a sense of movement and is known as asymmetry. (Cf. SYMMETRY).

Atelier (Fr.)   A workshop; an artist's or sculptor's studio.

Athletic School   See DIRECT PAINTING, SCHOOL OF.

Atlante   Male form of *caryatid* (q.v.).

Atmosphere   That quality in a work of art, usually of a literary or naturalistic tendency, that produces a sense of place, time or mood in the spectator (e.g. A Whistler "Nocturne," Madox Brown's "Chaucer at the Court of Edward III," Sickert's "Ennui").

Atmospheric Perspective   See AERIAL PERSPECTIVE.

Aureole (or Glory)   Distinguished from the *nimbus* (q.v.) in that it is a splendour of light surrounding not only the head but the whole figure.

Australian Aboriginal Art   There are two main categories of Australian primitive art, the naturalistic which is found in the drawings and paintings on bark in the north, *X-Ray drawings* (q.v.) and engravings on baobab seeds in the west, and the extremely symbolic drawings typical of Central Australia.

Autodidact French expression for the self-taught artist.

Auto-Lithograph (Direct lithograph) A print taken from a drawing made directly onto the stone or plate by the artist. The method, used most notably by Van Gogh, Toulouse-Lautrec and Cézanne, is being actively revived under this name in order to encourage the purchase of original works of art instead of more pretentious but usually less satisfactory colour reproductions. (See LITHO-GRAPHY).

Automatism In surrealist painting, the free movement of the hand and pencil or brush in drawing or painting, without the control of the conscious mind.

Aztec This name is usually applied to the inhabitants of the ancient Mexico city of Tenochtitlan, but it is more generally used for the culture of various independent groups inhabiting central Mexico from 1300 to the Spanish conquest in 1519-21. Aztec art is inseparable from Aztec religion of which a large feature was the cult of human sacrifice.

B

Bachiru (Jap.) A tinted ivory with a design engraved to reveal the natural light tone.

Bambino (It.) Representation of the Infant Christ.

Bambocciade (It.) A painting of common or rustic life grotesquely represented.

Barbizon School The name of a school of mid 19th cent. French landscape painters who made their home at Barbizon in the Fontainebleu forest and whose principle tenet was a return to nature. The movement, with which Corot was associated, included Millet, Rousseau, Troyon and Daubigny.

The principles of the school had a strong influence on art in the U.S.A. as a result of visits to France of two American painters, Hunt and La Farge.

Barbotine (Ceramics)   A slip or clay paste used in relief decoration of pottery.

Baroque   A word adapted from the Portuguese *barroco* or the Spanish *barrueco* meaning a rough or imperfect pearl. The term is used to-day for the art style of the period from about 1600-1720 which arose as the artistic accompaniment of the Jesuit Counter-Reformation. The Jesuits demanded a re-dedication of the arts in the service of the Church Militant, and in the building and decoration of their churches sought a style which would have a high propaganda effect by its emotional appeal and dramatic intensity.   The spirit of Baroque had already been adumbrated by three masters of the previous century, Michelangelo, Tintoretto and El Greco, all of whom had striven to dramatise composition, colour and content, and the Baroque painters of altarpieces and ceilings imitated the genuine spiritual turbulence of these three and produced a debased theatrical art. (Caravaggio, Domenicheno, Guido Reni, Ribera, Murillo).

In architecture, the result was a heavily and sometimes grotesquely ornamented style in which pillars, windows and recesses were added not for any structural purposes but to achieve a pleasing effect.

Examples of Baroque architecture are: the Church of the Invalides, Paris, designed by Mansart 1706. The Church of Sante Maria Della Salute, designed by Longhena. The Barberini Palace, Rome, designed by Bernini, Boromini and Maderna (See ROCOCCO).

Bas-Relief (Basso-Relievo)   Sculpture in low relief.

Batik (Malay)   A method of decorating fabrics in which the parts not to be coloured are impregnated with wax before dyeing. The wax is removed by boiling, and the process repeated for each colour used.

Bauhaus, The   A German educational institution and research centre for the training of architects, artists, industrial designers etc. Founded in Weimar in 1910 by Walter Gropius, it was transferred to Dessau in 1925 and closed by Hitler in 1932. The Bauhaus doctrine maintained that there could be no division between architecture, the fine arts and the applied arts, and that as they are all facets of man's creative artistic ability, the ultimate artistic goal should be "the compositely inseparable work of art, the great building." The Bauhaus applied an education principle which strove for the closest connection between art, science and technology. Gropius built round him a teaching staff which included Paul Klee, Moholy-Nagy, Marcel Breuer, Feininger and Wassily Kandinsky. In 1937 the New Bauhaus was opened in Chicago, to be known later as The Institute of Design, with a programme expanded on that of the original Weimar school.

Beauty   It has been said that there are as many conceptions of beauty as there are human beings. It would therefore serve no purpose to attempt a definition. But for anyone attempting to form a conception, the following points should be borne in mind. (1) Beauty is a matter of taste and opinion both of which are the product of experience. What is regarded as beautiful at one period of a person's life may not be so regarded at another.
(2) People may agree on what objects produce aesthetic experience and utterly disagree on a conceptual meaning.
(3) Beauty is not confined to art.

Biedermeier   This German word originally referred to a type of philistine (cheerful and honest but limited in outlook) and was applied to a phase of German art current between 1830 and 1860. The movement was a reaction against the later part of the Romantic Movement and produced scenes of simple peasant life, middle-class society and picturesque sentimental landscapes (e.g. the paintings of C. J. Milde, E. Engert, Karl Spitzweg, Gensler, Blechen and Rottman).

Biomorphic Art   A variety of Abstract Art opposed to the purely geometric or constructive, in which the shapes are reminiscent of, or even based on, organic forms. The term was originally applied by anthropologists to designs painted on pebbles by Palæolithic men of the Azilian Culture. Typical modern biomorphic art is that of Miro, Arp, Hélion and Erni.

Biscuit   Unglazed pottery. 'Biscuit' porcelain was manufactured in France during the late 18th cent. in order to simulate marble.

Bitumen   A mineral pitch obtained mainly from Egypt and used to a large degree by the painters of the early 19th cent. A most fugitive and slow-drying pigment, it is considered responsible for many of the failures amongst the painters of that period. Hiler remarks "Bitumen should be obsolete but it is unfortunately still procurable."

Black-Figured Vases   A type of terra-cotta pottery made in Greece during the 6th cent. B.C. Figures were painted in black glaze on the terra-cotta background and details were added by scratching. The style was perfected in Attica.

Blaue Reiter, The (Ger. The Blue Rider)   The title of a magazine edited by Franz Marc and Wassily Kandinsky which was to become "the mouthpiece of the new and serious ideas of our day," and was to effect a reconciliation between Art and the People. The name was extended to a group of artists which included Marc, Kandinsky, Macke, and Klee and which, inspired by Cubism, held exhibitions under the name of the Blaue Reiter Circle in most of the larger

German towns. Only the first issue of the magazine appeared, and the movement was brought to nothing by the outbreak of the 1914 war in which Marc was killed in 1916.

Blue Rose Group, The   A group of painters in Russia of the late 19th cent. which included Lanceres, Sepanov and Somov, who expressed the general European *fin de siecle* mood by a nostalgic and idealistic symbolism.

Body Colour   See WATERCOLOUR.

Boîte   A device conceived by the artist Marcel Duchamp consisting of a box which when opened up displays on screens facsimile reproductions in colour and half-tone of the artist's work. When manipulated the boîte unfolds before the spectator the whole of the work of the artist in retrospect presenting what is considered to be a composite portrait in aesthetic terms of the artist's personality.

Bologna, School of   School of painting founded towards the end of the 16th cent. in Bologna by Lodovico, Agostino and Anniable Carracci who followed in the footsteps of Raphael and Correggio in contrast to the prevailing realistic movement created by Caravaggio. The most famous work of this school is the painting of the gallery of Cardinal Farnese's palace in Rome.

Borough Group   This vital contemporary movement, named after the Borough Polytechnic, S.E. London, and which came into being in 1946, is composed of eleven young painters, who, under the leadership of the artist David Bomberg, are seeking a new method of expression. Dissatisfied with the tradition of academic art, and unable to subscribe to the purely formal preoccupations of abstract painting, they consider it necessary for the artist to enter into an almost mystical union with the subject of his painting, and to conceive with all his being a sense of its mass. In the words of Bomberg, the Group aims "to make more articulate the spirit in the mass." Constructive use of form and colour is not to be neglected, however, as there can be no worthwhile painting that is not founded on design and structure. In addition to its purely aesthetic function, the Group is socially conscious and is in fact a brotherhood in a very real sense, each member being prepared to help another in a case of necessity.

David Bomberg is a founder member of the *London Group* (q.v.), which he now declares devoid of its original adventurous spirit. The Borough Group, he hopes, will be to the London Group as the latter was to the *New English Art Club* (q.v.).

Bottega System   In Italy, the traditional method of training artists by apprenticeship in the bottega (workshop or studio) of a master. Beginning with the humbler tasks. the grinding of pigments etc., the pupil developed by way of painting backgrounds and other increasingly responsible assistance in completing a work. This system swelled the output of the master and while each work bore his signature many of them were almost entirely the work of pupils.

Boulle   See BUHL.

Broken Colour   In painting, the application of pigment in small strokes of different tints so that they merge at a distance.

Bronze   Sculpture in bronze is produced by casting from a mould taken from a clay original. Together with other forms of metal casting it constitutes that division of sculpture which is known as modelling as distinct from carving. The great merit of the medium lies in its suitability for the rendering of slender elongated forms (widely extended limbs, flying draperies etc.), and the surface of the metal readily lends itself to chasing.

The production of bronzes has formed an important aspect of the artistic activity of many cultures. The Greeks, who excelled in this form of sculpture, learned the technique from the Egyptians, and in turn passed it on to the Italians: but it is not until the advent of Donatello and thenceforward into the next century with Cellini that any high degree of skill was attained. After Cellini the medium was abused for the purpose of expressing flamboyant forms and exaggerated poses.

Bronze sculpture in Asia has a tradition of some 2,000 years, passing from Mesopotamia to Persia and thence to Greece and India. Knowledge of the craft was widely spread by Buddhist missionaries, and in India it is used not only for the representation of Buddhist figures but also for images of Hindu mythology where the material is particularly appropriate for rendering the many-armed figures. The Chinese have used bronze for ceremonial vessels rather than for statues with a superb effect which has been surpassed, however, by the Japanese whose work is equal to the finest Greek accomplishment.

In modern sculpture, mention must be made of the use of bronze by Epstein, Kolbe, Lachaise and Archipenko.

Brueghel   A family of Flemish painters with so many artistic members that it would seem useful to list them and indicate the characteristics of each.

Pieter the Elder (1520?-1569) known as "Peasant Brueghel" and "The Droll" painted scenes of peasant life, landscapes and biblical and fantastic scenes.

Pieter the Younger (1564?-1638?) son of above, known as "Hell" Brueghel because of paintings of infernal regions in addition to rural and genre subjects.

Jan the Elder (1568-1625) son of Pieter the Elder known as "Velvet" Brueghel, painted flowers as well as landscapes with mythological and biblical figures. He also painted backgrounds for Rubens and other figure painters.

Jan the Younger (1601-1678) son of the above, painted flowers and landscapes.

Ambrose (1617-1675) his brother, painted flowers and fruits.

Abraham (1631-1690) son of Jan the Younger, painted still-life in the Italian-Flemish style.

Jan Baptist (1670-1719) painter of flowers and fruits, was great grandson of Jan the Elder.

Bruges School   A school of art that flourished in Bruges in the 14th and 15th cents. The chief exponents were Hubert and Jan Van Eyck, Peter Christus, Hans Memlinc and Gheeraert David. The work of this school is often referred to as Flemish Primitive Art.

Buhl   English corruption of the name of the French cabinet maker, André Boulle (1642-1732), who invented a process of inlaying ebony with brass, silver, tortoiseshell, mother-of-pearl etc.

Buon Fresco   See FRESCO.

Burr   In engraving, the ridge of metal ploughed up by the graver or burin which is removed in line engraving in order to leave a clean line, but which is left on the plate in *drypoint* (q.v.) to which it imparts the softness characteristic of this medium.

Bushman Art   The art of the dwarf-like aboriginees of South Africa provides some of the finest examples of primitive art in the world, comparable only with the Palæolithic cave drawings of Dordogne in France and Altmira in Spain. Polychrome paintings and rock engravings and chippings of men and animals, executed in a highly naturalistic style and sometimes presented in extremely complicated poses, are found on cave walls and rock faces all over South Africa. This art seems to have been the product of the ancestors of the present aborigines, as the Bushman of to-day rarely produces anything more than crude geometric drawings on ostrich eggs.

Byzantine   Byzantium or Constantinople became the centre of a form of artistic activity about the 4th cent. A.D. which was later to become known as Byzantine Art. Graeco-Roman and Oriental forms were blended and adapted to express the Christianity newly adopted by the Roman Emperor Constantine, and the style reached its zenith in the reign of his successor Justinian (527-565).

The great successes of the Byzantine school were architectural. The building plan remained much the same as in the old Roman style, either round or Basilican in form, but the arch replaced the line of the architrave and the dome was adopted. The dome became the leading element in the new style and the principles of domical construction underwent far-reaching developments. Domes were placed over square apartments, whereas in the Roman style they had been placed only over circular apartments. Frequently, smaller domes were grouped round a large central dome which rose from four piers at the corner of a square as in the case of the Church of S. Sophia at Constantinople which, built by Justinian in 537, is regarded as the climax of Byzantine architecture.

Byzantine art took the form of mosaics, frescos, miniatures and panel paintings (icons), ivories, enamels, jewels and textiles, but mosaic was the medium most frequently used and the form of Byzantine art with which we are most familiar. The style was non-realistic, almost abstract, with no depth or perspective, and the emphasis was on colour with an abundance of gold.

C

Calcography   The art of drawing with chalks or
pastels.

Calligraphic In painting, a style of brushwork which has an expressive, linear quality as in, for example, many of the paintings of Henri Matisse.

Calligraphy The art of fine handwriting. In the present century there has been a revival of interest in this art led by Edward Johnston in England and Rudolf Koch in Germany.

Camaieu (Fr.) Painting in monochrome.

Camden Town Group A group of English painters founded in 1910 by Walter Sickert and his younger contemporaries, Harold Gilman, Charles Ginner and Spencer Gore, who were influenced by certain aspects of Post-Impressionism particularly, in the case of the younger men, by the work of Gauguin and Van Gogh, and who sought inspiration in grim and shabby streets. This group subsequently joined with other independent art societies to form the *London Group* (q.v.).

Cameo A precious stone cut in relief; consists generally of two or three colours, the upper cut in relief and the under forming the ground.

Camera Obscura Apparatus for reflecting an object onto a surface where it can be traced or drawn.

Canvas Canvas stretched on a châssis or wooden frame provides the most commonly used support for painting in oils. Despite the fact that authorities maintain that canvas is not a very suitable material from the point of durability over any considerable period of time, the majority of artists still find it the most sympathetic support upon which to work. This can be explained not only by the facility with which the pigment takes to the granular texture or "tooth" of the surface, but also by the satisfying relationship between the brush and a subtly resilient surface.

Caricature A drawing of a person in which the artist selects and emphasises unusual characteristics to the point of grotesqueness for the purpose of ridicule.

Carnations   A term, rarely used, to describe flesh-tints in painting.

Carolingian or Carlovingian Art   An epoch in art, named after Charlemagne, which began about 800 and ended about the middle of the 10th cent. During this time the antique tradition in the art of the south was transplanted into the north and became merged with northern tradition.   In architecture, the stone building of Greece and Rome was adapted to northern use, and the oblong or basilica plan began to be used in the construction of churches and larger buildings in northern Europe.   There is documentary evidence of many important murals of this period but none of them has survived.   Our knowledge of the art of this period is derived chiefly from a wealth of exquisitely illuminated manuscripts, some fine ivory carvings and some church furniture, reliquaries and chalices, of the finest workmanship.

Cartoccio (It.)   A little plate or scroll often found on Italian paintings upon which was inscribed the name of the artist or the subject of the portrait.

Cartoon   (1) A full scale drawing on paper to be used as a model for easel paintings, mural paintings, mosaics, stained glass and tapestry.

(2) Also used to describe drawings for reproduction in newspapers and magazines, usually humorous.

Cartouche   Architectural ornament in the form of a scroll on which armorial symbols are frequently carved.

Carving   That method of sculpture in which the artist works directly on a block of wood or stone with chisels.

Caryatid   A draped female figure serving as an architectural column, so called after the dancing women of the Greek town of Caryae.

Cassone (It.)   A large chest often decorated with painted panels.

Casting   In sculpture the process of duplicating a clay original in various metals by the use of moulds.   Various methods are used depending on whether one or more replicas are required.   In pottery, the manufacture of ware in moulds as opposed to its manufacture on the wheel.

Cavo-Relievo (It.)   Hollow relief.

Celadon Ware   A light grey-green glazed ware. The name derives from the colour of a coat worn by an 18th cent. French actor who played the part of a character called Celadon.

Celtic Art originated probably in the Middle Rhine area under the influence of Mediterranean cultures and reached its climax on the Continent during the 1st cent. B.C. during the last phase of the La Tène culture. The Celts in Europe were either Romanised in the West or Germanised in the East towards the end of this period, but the culture survived in England until the invasion of the Anglo-Saxons, and in Ireland until well into the Middle Ages.

Celtic art is manifested in the ornamentation of swords, shields, spearheads, bracelets etc. and is primarily geometric with an emphasis on line.   Much use is made of curved and spiral forms which become quite intricate in the later phases.   In the west the Celts worked with refinement and intricacy in enamel and red coral for the decoration of bronze objects such as shields and brooches.

Celtic style revived in Ireland in the 6th cent. and although displaced in the 7th and 8th cents. by the interlaced style, elements of the earlier stylistic phase remained apparent.

Central Asian Art (Turkestan)   By Central Asian Art is meant the art of the Buddhist kingdoms which flourished during the 3rd to 10th cents. along the caravan routes (skirting the north and south of the vast Taklamakan desert) from North West China to Afghanistan. The art is Sino-Indian in character, and in its earlier phases, at Miran in South East Turkistan, reveals much the same extension of Roman provincial forms as are found at Gandhara in North West India. The 5th and 6th cents. display Indo-Iranian influence in various styles, best typified by the wall paintings of the Thousand Buddha Caves at Kyzil on the Northern Silk Road. Two main phases are the earlier use of languorous forms and low colour range of the decoration in the Peacock Cave and the inarticulated figures and flat forms in vivid non-realistic colour of those in the Maya Cave. The paintings recovered from the Turfan Oasis in North East Turkestan and the wall paintings from the Bezäklik monastery are the best examples of the last phase of Central Asian Art and are almost completely Chinese in style. The Buddhist art of the region was brought to an end by the eastward advance of Mohammedanism.

Ceramics   The study of *pottery* (q.v.) as an art form.

Cerography   A method of painting which uses wax as a binder.

Chairs (Fr.)   Flesh colours as used in painting, sometimes referred to as *carnations*, which word, however, should only be used to describe the more delicate tints.

Chalk Drawing   Refers to a drawing executed in *crayon* or *pastel* (qq.v.).

Champlevé Enamel   A technique in enamel work usually applied to copper. The background not occupied by the design is hollowed out and the coloured, vitreous paste is applied to the space. (Cf. CLOISONNE ENAMEL).

Chance Configuration   In *Dadaism* (q.v.) the formation of patterns by experiments with such materials as threads, gauze etc., when blown or dropped onto a prepared piece of glass with the object of discovering forms independent of the hand.

Chantrey Bequest   A fund bequeathed to the Royal Academy in 1875 by Sir F. L. Chantrey, R.A. "for the purchase of works of painting and sculpture executed within the shores of Great Britain."

The fund is controlled by five trustees and works are purchased on the recommendation of two committees (for painting and sculpture) each composed of three members of the Academy and two members of the Tate Gallery Board.

Charcoal   Calcined woods of various kinds, particularly that of the vine, provide a sympathetic material for drawing, usually upon a coarse paper. Drawings with this medium are often shaded by the use of a "stump." While its use in the hands of a master can produce drawings of considerable merit, its inexperienced use will often result only in the meretricious. Charcoal is also often used for the preliminary drawing in oil painting.

Chasing   A method of ornamenting metal surfaces, particularly gold and silver, in which the design is embossed or hollowed out by means of steel punches.

Châssis   In painting, the frame on which a canvas is stretched. In sculpture, the revolving modelling stand on which the *armature* (q.v.) is placed.

Chef D'Ecole (Fr.)   Leader of a School, Group or Movement.

Chef-D'Oeuvre (Fr.)   A masterpiece.

Chiaroscurists   The name of a school of Italian painters led by Caravaggio (1565-1609) who developed a highly naturalistic style with the use of cold, hard lights and deep, black shadows.

Chiaroscuro   Italian word meaning light and dark (a similar word to pianoforte, meaning soft and loud) to describe those atmospheric effects which enable the painter to create the illusion that his subjects are on all sides surrounded by space.

Child Art   The study of child art, which began in the 80's of the last cent., was first regarded solely as an indication of the development of the individual child, and children's drawings were studied to arrive at generalisations which could be applied educationally.   But at the turn of the century, when the artistic mind began to focus on primitive art, it began to be recognised that child art had its own aesthetic significance.   Among other interesting observations, it was seen from the study of child art that the artistic development of mankind is repeated in the individual.   It was noticed that the powers of observation in children, particularly those under school age, are remarkably accurate, and they seize upon and reproduce the essential features of a scene or situation with remarkable clarity.   They have a disregard of perspective and frequently add details which, although not visible, they know to exist.   With no ulterior purpose or intellectual process intervening, the child produces its drawing simply as an emotional outlet.   Observations like these have had a direct influence on the practice of some modern artists in as much as they have attempted to re-create the naivety and fresh simplicity of the child's outlook.

Chinese Art   There is hardly any parallel between the art of China and that of the Western world. The Chinese approach to painting is a literary one of poetic evocation rather than representation or formal abstraction as in Western art, and the Chinese artist is bound by a set of strict rules (Cf. CHINESE SIX CANONS OF PAINTING) based upon calligraphic principles.   Each stroke of the brush is an end in itself and ideally possesses eight essential qualities: simplicity, strength, freshness, elegance, penetrative expressiveness, roundness and smoothness, solidness and stability, and ever-changing liveliness. Prime importance is given to the initial conception of a picture ("painting proceeds from the mind") and owing to the nature of the materials with which a Chinese artist works, ink, paper and silk, erasion, correction or "working over" is impossible, and the transcription has to be completed by a series of exact deliberate brush strokes unerringly applied.

Landscape ranks as the highest theme for the Chinese artist, and after landscape, flowers, trees, fruits and birds. Portraiture and the naturalistic representation of the human form plays a very small part.

Although colour is widely used with exquisite taste, it is used with the greatest reserve and caution and monochrome is considered the ideal form for rendering the essential qualities in nature, factors which, to the Chinese artist, transcend colour.

The Chinese artist has no desire for objective accuracy or factual description, and geometric perspective would destroy the artist's wish to achieve a continuously moving vision. "The shape of a mountain changes with every step one takes," says the Chinese painter, and he aims to show these changes in his work. To this end the Chinese have invented the long scroll form of painting, a horizontal painting, many feet long, which is unrolled gradually exposing only one small portion of the picture at a time. Each portion revealed must be complete in itself although there is a steady change of scene and mood which to the spectator is like going a journey or watching a drama.

But whereas the western mind is not easily attuned to Chinese painting it has no difficulty in recognising the supremacy of Chinese ceramics, an achievement which has been a continual source of inspiration to most European artists in this field.

The tradition of Chinese art has passed through

a number of distinct phases each produced during the rule of a particular dynasty. The most important from an artistic point of view have been treated under separate headings and are as follows:

Han Dynasty 206 B.C. - 220 A.D.

T'ang Dynasty 618 A.D. - 907 A.D.

Sung Dynasty 960 A.D. - 1280 A.D.

Yuan Dynasty 1280 A.D. - 1368 A.D.

Ming Dynasty 1368 A.D. - 1644 A.D.

Ch'ing (Manchu) Dynasty 1644 A.D. - 1912 A.D.

Chinese Six Canons of Painting   In Chinese painting certain basic rules laid down by Hsieh Ho (circa 500 A.D.) which have since been the guiding principles of Chinese painting up to the present day. The six canons are: "rhythmic vitality and life movement," "the structural use of the brush," "conformity with the object," "the application of colours according to their characteristics," "composition" and "transmission of style by copying and drawing."

Ch'ing Art   Ch'ing was the name assumed by the Manchu successors to the Ming Dynasty and Chinese art of this period (1644 A.D. - 1912 A.D.) is sometimes known as Manchu art. Painting of this period, although full of charm and executed with faultless technique, was fanciful and superficial and lacked the earnestness and sincerity of earlier and greater periods. It is, however, the style of Chinese painting which first became familiar in Europe and became the model for the eighteenth century fashion in 'chinoiserie'. Although the pottery of this period showed no great originality, it was unrivalled for technical perfection and exquisite finish and included the famous *K'ang Hsi ware* (q.v.).

Chinoiserie   A term used principally in 18th cent. France to cover the art of China, Japan and the Indies and the work of European imitators.   In modern usage it has come to mean European art influenced or inspired by east Asiatic art only.

Chou (Chinese)   Round wooden rod, usually with elaborately ornamented ends, around which a mounted painting is rolled.

Chryselephantine   Made of gold and ivory; applied to statues overlaid with gold and ivory.

Cinquecento   Italian for 500 and an abbreviation for *mil cinque cento*, 1500. Used to designate the years beginning with 1500, that is the 16th cent. Although referring to Italian art of the High and Late Renaissance, the term applies to a style rather than a time division, so it may also be applied to the work of artists of the previous century such as Leonardo da Vinci and Bramante.

Cinquecento style is the style of the Classical Renaissance which, beginning in the 15th cent. reached its climax in the latter part of the 16th cent. Ghiberti and Donatello were the pioneers in sculpture, Alberti and Brunelleschi in architecture, and Leonardo, Bramante, Titian and Correggio in painting.

Cire-Perdue (Fr. lost wax)   A method of casting bronzes used from very primitive times. Briefly, a clay model is covered with a layer of wax and the whole enclosed in a clay or plaster shell, a tube having been inserted at either end. When the molten metal is poured through the upper tube the wax is melted and flows away through the lower tube, its place being taken by the bronze. The shell is then broken off and the model removed.

Classic Art   That form of art where the artist is principally concerned with the construction of a work based upon formal principles rather than with the expression of a subjective mood as in the case of *Romantic Art* (q.v.). Classic art is based upon the art of Classical Greece (See GREEK ART) with its discipline and predominantly intellectual appeal.

All art may be roughly divided into Romantic and Classic, and the history of art consists largely of a succession of fluctuations in favour of one attitude or the other. The expression *"Architectural Art"* (q.v.) has been coined by the critic R. H. Wilenski as a more appropriate term for classic art which he considers to be based on "architecture as typical art."

Claude Lorraine Glass   A small reflecting surface for use chiefly in landscape sketching, a common implement of the studios of the 17th and 18th cents. By means of a black convex glass the large scene was reduced to a small area eliminating much of the detail.

Cleaning   The question of whether the pictures in the National Gallery ought or ought not to be cleaned has raised a controversy three times in the history of the Gallery, in 1846, 1936 and again in 1947.
Those in favour of cleaning maintain that it is desirable to see the picture as the artist originally painted it by the removal of varnish and dirt, and the critics assert that time in the shape of this same varnish and dirt has mellowed and enhanced the artist's original conception.
The 1947 Exhibition of Cleaned Pictures aroused a certain amount of resentment, but nothing compared with the cleanings of 1846 and 1936 which were clumsily done and caused some damage to the works. Public opinion is now largely on the side of the authorities in preferring its art treasures clean.

Cloisonné Enamel   A technique in enamel work. The design is applied to the background, usually gold, by a number of fences in thin gold, and the interstices or "cloisons" are then filled in with vitreous pastes of various colours. This method was used in enamels of Byzantine origin.

31

Cloisonnisme   A French word for the style in painting, used most notably by Gauguin and Rouault, where emphasis is given to forms in a picture by surrounding them with deep, lead-like lines.

Collage (Fr. a pasting)   A picture or visual arrangement made in part or entirely of pasted pieces of paper, wallpaper, illustrations, photographs or any other textured or figured material. The *Cubists* (q.v.) were the first to use this method as a serious form of expression, but the idea was adopted and developed more widely by the *Dadaists* and *Surrealists* (qq.v.). Whereas the Cubist use of collage was devoted to formal and decorative purposes, the Surrealists used the process for the arrangement of magazine and catalogue cuttings etc. to express an extreme form of *associationism* (q.v.).

Cologne, School of   A general name for the schools of painting centred in Cologne during the 14th, 15th and 16th cents.

Colour   Dr. Herbert Read recognises four uses of colour in a work of art. (1) Natural Colour. Colour is this sense together with light and shade, completes the "likeness" of a picture. (2) Heraldic Colour. The conventional use of colour governed either by established rules (e.g. church stained glass) or primitive symbolism (e.g. green tree, blue sea, yellow sand). (3) Harmonic Colour. The use of a scale of colours in which each is considered in relationship to the rest. A dominant colour in the painting is selected to which the others are scaled up or down within a restricted range. (4) Pure Colour. Colour used for its own sake. Taken in their purest intensity, colours are built up into patterns of contrasts. The main object being decorative, colour is thus reduced to its most direct sensuous appeal.

See INDUCED COLOUR, LOCAL COLOUR, REFLECTED COLOUR.

Colour Perspective   See AERIAL PERSPECTIVE.

Command of Hand   In the art of handwriting, ornamentation composed of pen strokes and done directly and freely without preliminary drawing.

Complementary Colour   The three primary colours in pigments are red, blue and yellow. Any other colour is a mixture of two or all of the primaries in varying degrees. The *complementary* to any given colour is a mixture of those primaries lacking in its composition. Thus, the complementary to red is green (blue and yellow mixed) and blue is complementary to orange (red and yellow mixed). A greenish grey is a mixture of yellow, blue and a little red, and its complementary therefore is a reddish brown, a mixture of all three primaries with red predominating.

Composition   The arrangement of form and colour in a work of art, often found by intricate analysis to obey certain precise geometric rules which Leonardo, Picasso, certain peasant potters and, in fact, all artists of sensibility break to fit their own peculiar genius.

Concrete Art   An alternative name for abstract art preferred by Wassily Kandinsky. To the purist, the expression "abstract art" is a misnomer because the word can only be accurately applied to an intangible idea. The act of painting gives substance to an idea, and the result, so far from being abstract, is actually its opposite and, in Kandinsky's opinion, is more accurately described as "concrete."

Constants   "*Organic* constant universal forms" found in nature (such as the egg, sea shells etc.) and "*Mechanic* constant universal forms" that is to say the type-forms, man- and machine-made things (such as wheels, bowls and jugs), both of which the *Purists* (q.v.) used as the basic motifs for their compositions.

33

Constructivism   A Russian movement in abstract art developed by Pevsner and Gabo from *Suprematism* (q.v.). Constructivism " . . . . rejected the painted canvas entirely and resorted to the materials of the engineer and architect." In the big 'Constructivist exhibition of 1920 (the date of the movement's Manifesto) were displayed abstract figures built from bits of pasteboard and complex arrangements of wood and metal. This movement, which extended to the design of theatre settings, finally merged in 1932 with the Paris group of *Abstraction-Création* (q.v.). Other artists associated were Tatlin, Moholy-Nagy, Malevich, Lissitzky and Rodchenko.

Conté   A kind of black crayon named after the original makers, Conté of Paris.

Contemporary Art Society   This Society was founded in 1910 to give "encouraging patronage to living artists and to enable their work to be seen where it has previously been inadequately represented in the public galleries." The C.A.S. has been directly responsible for the Tate Gallery acquiring the first work of many artists who are now famous. Membership is £1 p.a. for which there are certain privileges. Assist. Sec., Denis Mathews, Esq., The Tate Gallery, Millbank, S.W.1.

Content   The subject matter of a work of art (either in a literary or a representative sense) as opposed to the *form* by which it is given expression.

Contour   The outline of a form: the line that bounds.

Contrapposto (It.)   Relationship of contrasted masses.

Conventional Art   The simplification of forms in order to achieve a decorative effect. A conventional drawing usually confines itself to straight lines and simple curves.

34

Conversation Piece   A form of *genre painting* (q.v.) in which a group is represented of figures linked by some slight thread of common interest.   Hogarth, who might be said to be its inventor, best exemplifies this type of painting.

Corbel (Fr. a raven, hence a beak-like projection)   A block of stone or wood projecting from a wall to support or help support a projecting feature.

Corbie, School of   A Carolingian school of illuminators and miniature painters which produced the famous Codex Aureus, written by the brothers Beringar and Liuthard to the order of Charles the Bald in 879.

Correct Drawing   A term used by artists to denote specific information in terms of free-hand drawing.

Cosmato Work   The marble work of the Cosmati families who flourished in and around Rome from the late 12th to the early 14th cents.

Counterchange   In a repetitive pattern or design, the process of alternately reversing the colours or motifs. E.g., in a diaper pattern, the first section might contain a gold fleur-de-lis on a blue ground and the following section a blue fleur-de-lis on a gold ground etc.   Motifs can be similarly arranged in alternating relationships.

Counter Relief   A method of sculptural relief, invented by the Russian Constructivist, Tatlin, executed in contrasting materials.

Crackle   In pottery the calculated fracturing of the glaze on vessels when firing in order to produce a desired effect.   This should not be confused with 'crazing' which is accidental. Crackle can be so finely controlled by the mixture of certain kinds of clay in the glaze that bands of alternately wide and small meshed crackle can appear on the same vessel.

Crayon   Pigments bound, usually by wax, to form a hard stick.   Extremely suitable for rapid sketching, it has been used by many masters with fine effect.

Crazing ('Cer.)   In pottery, the accidental fracturing of the glaze.   Although unintentional, oriental potters frequently regard this as an enhancement of the beauty of the ware, as in fact they do many accidental effects of the firing.

Cretan-Minoan   The name of an artistic culture on the Island of Crete which flourished from about the end of the 3rd millenium until about 1200 B.C. Recent excavations have discovered skilfully built palaces decorated with lively colourful frescos, a number of exquisite figurines in glazed terra-cotta, ivory and ivory and gold, metal work in the form of gold cups, with floral patterns and hunting scenes worked in repoussé and a number of bronze daggers with damascened scenes of lion hunts in gold and silver.   The work of this early but highly developed culture was exported throughout the eastern Mediterranean and exercised a great influence on the island and mainland cities of Greece.

Crevé (Etch.)   A condition where the acid has widened and broken down the areas between lines so that they print a grey and faint impression.

Crocket   An ornament, usually in the form of carved foliage, found on the sloping edge of a flying buttress, gable, pinnacle, etc. of a Gothic building.

Cubism   The name of a geometric-abstract style of painting and sculpture begun by Picasso and Braque in 1907 largely as a result of a remark made by Cézanne in a letter published that year in which he said "You must see in nature the cylinder, the sphere and the cone."   This, together with a growing interest in African Negro sculpture, led Picasso and Braque to experiment in the reduction of natural forms to their fundamental geometric shapes. Picasso's *Young Ladies of Avignon* of 1907 is considered the first Cubist picture, and his *Head* of 1909 the first Cubist sculpture.

This first phase, known as "analytical cubism" was followed by the development known as "simultaneity" in which attempts were made to present different views of an object in a single composition. At the same time colour and the third dimension were eliminated resulting in two-dimensional, monochromatic designs. About 1913 the "synthetic" or *"collage"* (q.v.) method was developed in which pieces of paper and other materials in addition to paint were used in the composition of pictures. Cubism in this form was continued by Picasso until 1925 when he began to turn to surrealistic forms of expression, and by Braque until the 1930's.

Other outstanding cubist painters are: Gleizes, Metzinger, Léger, Delaunay, Picabia, Gris, Jeanneret (now Le Corbusier), Ozenfant, Duchamp, La Fresnaye, Villon, and Marcoussis.

Among sculptors, the following might be termed cubists owing to the highly abstract nature of their work: Picasso, Brancusi, Belling, Lipchitz, Laurens, Boccioni and Archipenko. (See ABSTRACT ART, CONSTRUCTIVISM).

Cycladic Art   The Pre-Hellenic art of the Aegean Islands.

D

Dadaism (Fr. Dada — a hobby horse)   This name epitomizes the aims of an artistic and literary movement that became a sensation in Berlin, Paris and other continental cities in the 1920's. The impulse behind Dadaism was disillusionment and disgust with a society which could allow such a holocaust as World War I, and it expressed itself by a cynical and violent reaction to the conventional in the arts — a sort of cultural counterpart of political anarchy. Dadaist methods usually took the form of geometrical diagram pictures and compositions fabricated out of any old thing that came to hand: buttons, bits of tin, paper, textiles, bus tickets, pieces of wire, cotton reels etc. The results were fantastic childish concoctions, "the symbolic results of uninhibited subconscious creativeness," and were classified under a number of strange headings: Rubbish, Constructions, Fatagagas, "Merz" (i.e. rubbish) Pictures, Ready Made Objects, Exquisite Corpses, Collages, Rayographs.

Members held numerous exhibitions, published proclamations and manifestos, published several short-lived periodicals, staged plays and poetry readings, held soirées and festivals, opened a Dada night-club in Berlin and founded a newspaper in Cologne. The movement lasted in Germany until 1920 and in France until 1922.

The chief exponents of the movement were Tristan Tzara, Marcel Duchamp, Hans Arp, Marcel Janco, Huelsenbeck, Hugo Ball, Francis Picabia, Man Ray, André Breton, Philippe Soupault, Guillaume Apollinaire, Louis Aragon, Max Ernst and Kurt Schwitters.

Dadaism was undoubtedly a forerunner of Surrealism. But where Surrealism is a conscious and deliberate presentation of subconscious and dream-like images, Dadaism was little more than a wild, haphazard effort to be sensational and shocking at all costs. Many of the Dadaist painters became Surrealists after 1924.

Daguerrotype   An early method of photography invented by the French painter L. J. M. Daguerre in 1839. The Daguerrotype exercised a strong influence on the work of the mid 19th cent. English painters in so far as they tried to reproduce in paint the wealth of naturalistic detail shown in a photograph, e.g. The Pre-Raphaelites.

Damascene   (1) The ornamentation of iron or steel with inlaid designs in gold or silver.

(2) A watered pattern produced by

forging rods of iron which have been welded together and twisted.

Both processes are practised in Persia and India and the name derives from Damascus where the art originated and where the famous blades of that name were made.

Decorated Style   The second Gothic style of architecture in use in England during the 14th cent. The name is somewhat ill-bestowed, as the style is not so richly ornamented during this period as the subsequent *Perpendicular Style* (q.v.).

Decorative Art   Art which has for its principle purpose the enlivening or embellishment of a wall, a book page, a piece of pottery etc. as distinct from art which produces works which are ends in themselves.

Degenerate Art (Ger. Entarte Kunst)   Hitler dismissed and suppressed most modern art as " political and cultural anarchy " and " art bolshevism." An exhibition of modern art (for adults only) was opened in Munich in 1937 under the name of Entarte Kunst and later toured all over Germany to display the decadence of modernism and to serve as a warning. Among the artists represented were: Otto Dix, Emil Nolde, Franz Marc, Paul Klee, Marc Chagall, Oskaar Kokoschka, Karl Hofer, Wassily Kandinsky, Max Beckmann, George Grosz, Lydnel Feininger, Lovis Corinth and Paula Modersohn-Becker.

Hitler also "purified" the German Art Galleries by removing and selling outside Germany works by Van Gogh, Gauguin, Picasso, Derain, Barlach, Modigliani and Lehmbruck.

Del.   Abbreviation of Delineavit (Latin 'he drew'). Used on engravings to indicate the name of the artist responsible for the original drawing.

Derivative Art   This term applies to the work of unoriginal popular artists who derive their ideas from some established master or style of painting, or even to the work of original artists who continue to repeat themselves in the style of their earlier successes.

At the present time, for example, popular taste has at last assimilated the once revolutionary ideas of Impressionism, and therefore any painter who turns out imitations of this style is reasonably assured of an appreciative audience.

Descriptive Art   Art which has for its principle purpose the recording of scenes and objects of social, historical or scientific interest.   Original, significant work within this category has become increasingly rare since its utilitarian function was superseded by the camera.   The recording of battle and hospital scenes during the last two wars, however, where an emotional response impossible for the camera was necessary, has produced a number of descriptive works of some value.

Design   Properly, design is the planning, by means of a sketch, model or cartoon, of a projected work of art preliminary to its final execution.   In painting, however, the term is more generally used to describe the formal pattern in which the various elements of line, tone, colour etc. are arranged, and in this sense design might be considered synonymous with *composition* (q.v.).   The term is also used in another sense in decorative art to describe the pattern or ornament applied to a plain surface.

De Stijl Group (Dutch: The Style)   A Dutch geometric-abstract movement in art and architecture begun by Theo Van Doesburg in 1917 and which included Piet Mondriaan, Vantongerloo, the sculptor, and two architects, Oud and Rietveld. This movement, which lasted until 1931, emphasised the use of rectangles and primary colours and had a considerable influence on commercial and industrial arts.

Diaper   A repeat pattern of geometric or floral motif used to decorate a whole surface.

Die Brücke (Ger. The Bridge)   A group of German painters founded in Dresden in 1905 to develop the *Expressionism* (q.v.) of Edvard Munch. The founders were Ernst Ludwig Kirchner, Erich Heckel and Karl Schmidt-Rottluff, and Emil Nolde was for a time associated with them.   Savage art and the work of Van Gogh were the two most important sources of inspiration. Die Brücke collapsed in 1913 having served its purpose of launching the German Expressionist Movement.

Die Neue Sachlichkeit (Ger. The New Objectivity) A phrase coined by Dr. Hartlaub, Director of Mannheim Art Gallery, to describe the art of a small group of post 1914-18 war artists which included Max Beckman, Otto Dix and George Grosz.   These artists expressed the German post-war resignation and cynicism in war pictures of incomparable grimness, but were saved from a merely negative attitude, by a genuine enthusiasm for immediate reality "the result of a desire to take things entirely objectively on a material basis without immediately investing them with ideal implications".

Diptych   An altarpiece consisting of two hinged panels usually painted or sculptured in relief.

Direct Painting, School of   An American school of landscape painters of the late 19th cent. with which are connected the names of Redfield, Symons, Wendt, Schofield, Lie, Dougherty and Harrison, who revolted against the lack of contour in Impressionist painting, and who portrayed solidity by strong modelling and bold brushwork. They were also known as the *Athletic School* or the *Sculpturesque Painters*.

Distemper   A method of painting in which the pigment is bound by glue or size and diluted with water.   The method is rarely used for studio painting, but it is the usual method for scene painting in theatres.

Distortion   Distortion is the artist's departure from exact imitation dictated by his preoccupation with form or his desire to give expression to the ideal. The latter use of distortion as in Greek sculpture (the unnaturally straight line of nose and forehead and the exaggerated length of leg) is readily understood; but the extreme cases of distortion in much modern art can only be understood in the light of the artist's fundamental purpose. One such purpose might be briefly described as the artist's desire to recreate natural forms in rhythmic terms of form and colour. The modern artist who is not concerned with naturalistic representation has little use for the outward appearance of things, his object being the creation of form rather than imitation, and distortion contributes to this end.

Divisionism is the methodical process introduced by Seurat and the *Neo-Impressionists* (q.v.) by which a picture was built up by a careful geometric integration of its elements, line, form, and colour, to obtain a composition in which all the parts were distinguishably separate and which yet merged optically. The term should not be confused with *Pointillism* (q.v.) which was merely the method by which the paint was applied.

Douanier, The (Fr. Customs Officer)   Soubriquet of the French artist Henri Rousseau (1844-1910) who earned his living in that capacity.

Double-Action Drawing   A device in drawing, used by the Neo-Surrealists, Cubists and Futurists, in which the upper part of a figure is represented in one attitude and the lower part in another. The Futurists used it to convey an idea of movement, and the idea was adopted by Picasso for formal reasons and developed by him to a point where the figures were actually disintegrated and re-combined into a new design.

Drawing   The art of drawing is the use of pencil, pen, chalk or brush, either alone or in combination, to note an impression, to make a detailed study or design a projected work.   The draughtsman is mainly concerned with the expression of form by means of *line* (q.v.) and light and shade, and in his hands these become symbols for the representation of nature (Cf. PAINTING).

The aesthetic value of a drawing lies mainly in the rhythmic quality of its line and the intimate insight which it gives into the working of the artist's mind.   Drawing is, in fact, a form of note-taking practiced by the artist to express his own innermost thoughts or his reflections on the outside world. Although this process is often auxiliary to the artist's function as a painter, the two arts are, nevertheless, quite distinct.   As Dr. Herbert Read has expressed it "we do not regard shorthand as a useful preparation for the art of writing".

Dresden China   Porcelain made by Johann Friedrich Böttger of Dresden at Meissner in Saxony, who first grasped the principle of vitrification involved in imitation of the Chinese product.   Dresden China, or Saxon China as it is known in France, enjoyed a vogue for forty years during the early 18th cent. and is still collected with enthusiasm.   The type-product is, of course, the well-known 'Dresden Shepherdess'.

Drypoint   A method of engraving in which the graver is used directly on the plate without the use of an acid.   The beauty of this method is produced by the burr which is thrown up by the tool on each side of the channel and which is not removed as in the case of ordinary line engraving.   The effect of this in printing is to produce the velvety line characteristic of this medium.   As the burr soon wears away in printing, only a very limited edition (approximately thirty copies) can be made.

Duccento (It. two hundred)   Used to describe 13th cent. Italian painting.

Dusseldorf, School of   A style of painting connected with the Academy of Art at Düsseldorf (Ca. 1830-1850) which was one of the centres of *Biedermeier Art* (q.v.). The style of the School, in addition to having the genre characteristics of Biedermeier Art, displayed some of the heroic tendencies of the current romanticism of German art.

E

Early Christian Art   The early Christians adopted the contemporary Roman style in painting for the depiction of Christian themes, and practically all that has survived of this period is to be found in the catacombs beneath Rome. Roman art of that period, with its purely materialistic conceptions, was ill-suited for the expression of the mysticism of the new religion and these paintings are therefore of little aesthetic interest. It was not until Byzantium with its eastern influences became the centre of the Roman world and Christianity became the official religion that a distinctly Christian style of art was formed.

Early English Style   The first Gothic style of architecture used in England during the 13th cent.

Earthenware   One of the two main divisions of pottery, being clay baked to a temperature sufficient to render it hardened but leaving it still porous, thereby requiring the addition of glaze in order to make it impervious to liquids. (Cf. STONEWARE).

Ebauche (Fr. sketch, rough draft)   In oil painting, the underpainting or first coat of the actual picture next to the *ground* (q.v.). The ébauche is not always used, but when it is, it should have special qualities and purposes as, for example, the use of conventionally agreed upon colours. The underpainting is sometimes painted in monchrome tonal values and coloured in the final painting by the use of glazes. Technically, the ébauche should have a low oil content in order to enable the subsequent paintings to adhere properly.

Echoppé An early form of etching needle with a bevelled point which made a line that varied considerably in thickness, thus imitating steel engraving.

Eclecticism In art, eclecticism describes the work of an original artist who, while strongly influenced by the work of other artists, schools or traditions, is yet able to express his own personal vision.

Eclectics The name of the first European Academy of Art founded by the brothers Carracci in the late 16th cent. in Italy. The school was formed to preserve the main tradition of Renaissance art in opposition to the Baroque nature of the later work of Michelangelo from whose earlier work, together with that of Raphael and Correggio, the Eclectics derived the inspiration for their style.

Ecole De Paris (Fr. School of Paris) Paris is traditionally the centre of the art world, and the School of Paris refers therefore to the work and ideas of the cosmopolitan community of artists living and working there. Historically, however, the term refers more particularly to the leaders of the modern movement in the important years between the two World Wars.

Ecole Des Beaux Arts A well-known endowed school of the fine arts in Paris founded in 1648.

Ecorché (Fr. a flayed figure) An anatomical painting or sculpture with skin removed to display muscular construction.

Einfühlung See EMPATHY.

Elements of Painting The *material elements* of a painting are (1) The *Support* upon which the painting is made. (2) The *ground* which renders the support suitable to receive the painting. (3) The pigments of which the painting is composed.

The *abstract* or *physical elements* of a picture are line, tone (light and shade), mass (or volume), space (which is negative mass) and colour.

Embossing The art of producing raised patterns on metal, leather or similar materials. The term was originally applied to patterns beaten out from the reverse side of the materials, but to-day the word principally refers to the production of raised impressions by means of engraved dies or plates as in embossed note-paper headings.

Emotive Fragment A phrase coined by the critic R. H. Wilenski to describe the source of inspiration or "jumping off" point of most emotional or romantic art. In using this phrase the critic aims at a distinction between the fragmentary and emotional incentive behind the work of a romantic artist, and the classical artist's primary concern with formal harmony and unity.

Empathy A word coined from Greek sources to translate the German *Einfühlung* which means literally "feeling into". Empathy is the basis of modern 'psychological' theories of art in contrast to the less subtle 'objective' theories. The best-known exponent of the theory, Theodore Lipps, uses the word to describe the identification of the self with the form of a work of art and the resultant emotion.

Enamel The application of a thin coat of glass to certain metals to which it is fused by raising both to a considerable temperature.

Encaustic An almost obsolete method of painting with vehicles including wax as the chief ingredient.

After application by means of a spatula or "cestrum," the pigment was heated by passing red-hot charcoal in a "cauterium" all over the painting a few inches from the surface, thus melting the wax and producing an homogenous surface. Hence the name, which is from the Greek "burnt in".

Engraving   The art of decorating wood, metal or stone with incised lines.

Engraving is mainly concerned with the preparation of metal plates for reproducing designs by the intaglio or recess process, i.e. the incising of lines which, when charged with ink, are transferred to paper under pressure. (See AQUATINT, ETCHING, LINE ENGRAVING, MEZZOTINT, WOOD ENGRAVING).

Entasis   The slight swelling in the shaft of a column which corrects the optical illusion of concavity in the sides when several columns are used together.

Equipoised Sculpture   Normally, sculpture is concerned to express some relationship with the earth's surface, i.e. since it rests upon a base, the subject has either to recline horizontally, stand vertically or take up some oblique position. The conception of an equipoised sculpture, on the other hand, disposes of this gravitational influence and postulates the self-contained and independent volume, concerning itself only with problems of volume and material.

Such a conception is a purely theoretical one, the realization of which might only come about by the use of magnetic devices or remote electrical control. In practice, however, the *Constructivists* (q.v.) (Pevsner, Gabo, Moholy-Nagy) have made experiments depending upon illusion in which glass and invisible wires were used to support the sculptures, giving the impression that they were in fact existing independent of the law of gravity.

Esquisse   French expression for a preliminary sketch for a projected work of painting, sculpture or architecture.

Etching   An engraving process which makes use of an acid to incise a design onto a metal plate. The plate is first covered with an acid-resisting ground upon which the design is drawn with a needle to the depth of the plate. The plate is then immersed in acid which bites into the metal where the ground has been removed. The depth of the bite can be controlled by removing the plate and re-applying the ground over those lines where a delicate effect is required and re-immersing to increase the strength of the remaining lines.

Etruscan Art   The art of the civilization centred in Tuscany during the 7th to 1st cents. B.C. It was mainly Hellenistic in style but lacked the spirit of its Greek models. The archaic period, 600 to 450 B.C., is notable for its abundance of terra-cotta images, sandstone reliefs and vivid tomb paintings, all of which reveal an exuberance of feeling. This was followed in the 5th and 4th cents. by a period of uninspired imitation of classical Greek art. During the 3rd and 2nd cents. B.C. Etruscan art shared in the rise of provincial Hellenism in Italy and failed to capture the intellectual and spiritual quality of Greece, expressing instead sometimes an aggressive and at other times an introspective emotionalism. In the light of modern art, Etruscan painting and sculpture are esteemed for their exceptional vitality which arises from richness of pattern and extraordinary strength of colour, all rendered with high technical ability.

Euston Road Group   A group of English painters founded just before the last war and headed by Victor Passmore and William Coldstream. The group sought to revive the ideals of *Impressionism* (q.v.) as a reaction against the amateurish sensationalism of contemporary French painting, and under the sociological influence of Graham Bell, the members of the group looked for their themes in the more sordid aspects of urban life. The group dissolved during the latter part of the war.

Evangeliar   A type of illuminated manuscript containing the Four Gospels in unabridged form which is of considerable artistic importance because the best examples display mediaeval art in its finest aspects. They are richly ornamented and illustrated, and probably the most famous example is the 8th cent. "Book of Kells" in Trinity College Library, Dublin.

Expressionism   Expressionism in art is where the artist is principally concerned with giving form to intimate and personal emotions, and describes the feeling in European painting which rejected the objective naturalism of the Impressionist movement in favour of a subjective imaginative approach. For this reason, Expressionism in France was the principle which inspired Post-Impressionism and subsequent movements under the leadership of Van Gogh, Gauguin, Matisse and Rouault. But it is in the German Expressionist Movement (Expressionismus) that the attitude found its fullest development amongst members of the *Die Brücke* group (1905) and the *Blaue Reiter Circle* (1911) (qq.v.). German Expressionism varied from the violent distortion of natural forms of Nolde and Kokoschka to the symbolism and abstraction of Klee and Kandinsky.

F

Facet-Cubism   An early phase of Cubism (1909-11) in which Braque and Picasso attempted to symbolize space by the use of advancing and receding planes. This was, in fact, an extension of the earlier experiments of Cézanne, but moved towards a greater degree of abstraction than was ever in that artist's mind.

Factura   A Russian form of *collage* (q.v.) developed mainly by the Constructivists, in which various materials were imposed onto the canvas principally to exploit their textural values.

Faience   A word derived from the Italian town of Faenza and applied generally to glazed earthenware and porcelain.

Famille Verte, Rose, Jaune, Noir   Famille Verte is a variety of Chinese enamelled porcelain of the K'ang Hsi reign (1662 - 1722) which has earned the name because of the predominance of green in the palette of colours used in its decoration. Famille Rose became popular in the succeeding reign of Yung Chêng (1723 - 35) in which the translucent colour of Famille Verte gave way to a palette of opaque enamels dominated by a range of rose pinks. Famille Noir and Famille Jaune are groups of lesser importance so named for similar reasons.

Fatamid Art   The Islamic art of the Fatamides Dynasty which reigned in Egypt during the 10th, 11th and 12th cents. A.D. In architecture, the style of the period favoured massive construction with delicate surface ornament which became the pattern for the finest West-Islamic architecture. Examples are found in Cairo in the mosques of al-Azhar, al-Hakim and al-Akmar, and in the gates of Bab al-Futuh, Bab al-Nasr and Bab Zuwayla.

Fauves (Fr. wild beasts)   A name first contemptuously applied to a group of French artists who exhibited at the Salon d'Automne in Paris in 1905. The distinctive feature of these paintings was the violent use of bright colour and a contempt for academic representation. Matisse was the leader of the movement, which included Marquet, Rouault, Vlaminck, Derain, Dufy and Braque, and he was directly inspired by his study of Byzantine mosaics, Persian and eastern art generally, and by the prevailing interest in negro sculpture. The Fauves also derived considerable inspiration from the work of Van Gogh and Gauguin.

Figuratif (Fr. Figurative) Painting   French name for representative painting as opposed to non-figuratif, or abstract, painting.

Figurine   Any small modelled or sculptured figure.

Fine Art   Fine art is that art which is principally concerned with the production of works of aesthetic significance as distinct from useful or *applied art* (q.v.) which is utilitarian in intention.

Flambé (Cer.)   The irregular application of glaze, usually by splashing, which is sometimes found on Chinese porcelain.

Flashed (Cer.)   Discolouration in pottery caused by direct contact with flame in the firing.

Flat-Pattern Cubism   A term first used by the critic R. H. Wilenski to describe that phase of Cubism where lines, shapes and colours were disposed upon the canvas "without any attempt to suggest recession into space behind the canvas".

Florentine School   A name applied to the artistic products of the City of Florence from the 13th to the 16th cents. The Florentine is generally held to be the leading school of the Italian Renaissance. The artists of that city, while preserving strong individualities, shared a common regard for the classic conception of the human form.

During the 13th and 14th cents. the School was Gothic in spirit and was dominated first by Cimabue and later by his great successor Giotto (1266/76-1377). In the 15th cent. the Gothic tradition was maintained by Fra Angelico (1387-1455), while Massaccio (1401 ca-1428) introduced a realistic tendency. Fra Fillipo Lippi (1406 ca - 1469) and Domenico Ghirlandajo (1499-1494) led a group of descriptive painters, and the close of the cent. saw the singular achievement of Botticelli (1444/45-1510) and the rise of Leonardo da Vinci (1452-1519). The 16th cent. the period known as the High Renaissance, saw the full flowering of the Florentine genius in the work of Michelangelo (1475-1564) and Raphael (1483-1520) and the later and greatest work of Leonardo. The School also dominated Italy in sculpture in the 15th cent. with Donatello (1386-1466) and Verocchio (1435-1488).

Folk Art   See PEASANT ART.

Foredge Painting   Paintings made on the foredges of books.

Foreshortening   In perspective, any distance which recedes from the eye is apparently diminished. (See PERSPECTIVE). Foreshortening is the means whereby an artist renders this effect, e.g. a limb or body in figure painting or a receding road in a landscape.

Form   The structural element in a work of art or the means whereby the artist's vision is given shape. Except in theory, form and content are inseparable, but in much modern art, particularly *abstract art* (q.v.), the intention is to present the maximum amount of form with the minimum amount of *content* (q.v.).

Formalism   Formalism in art is the representation of the formal aspects of a subject devoid of its content, i.e., the artist uses natural shapes to achieve a pleasing composition without reference to the deeper significance of the objects represented. Formalism is the basis of much decorative art and is characteristic of those periods in art where over-preoccupation with form has drained the artist of any emotional response. There might appear to be some confusion between *Formalism* and *Abstraction* in art, but where the abstract artist attempts to express the essential formal quality of his subject, the formal artist is merely concerned with the superficial arrangement of shapes.

Found Object   A Surrealistic term to describe objects usually found in nature, stones, twigs, roots, driftwood etc., singled out for the fantastic or aesthetic configurations imposed upon them by the accidents of nature.   Such objects are frequently treated in some way and are then known as *found objects interpreted* or *assisted*.

Fractional Concept   In some early and primitive art forms, and in the drawings of young children, an object is sometimes rendered as a combination of its various elements rather than as a whole.   The well-known wall paintings of Ancient Egypt provide a typical example where the frontal view of the eye is shown on a profile of a head, and side views of the limbs are attached to a front view of the body.

Frame   The frame of a picture (or the boundaries of the canvas) is regarded as an essential element in a composition, and all elements within the picture must bear relationship to it.   Composition within the frame is a fundamental problem for the artist who has to select from nature, which is panoramic and normally unbounded, a section which will fit — if necessary by alteration and transposition — within the imposed limitations.

French Method   See WATERCOLOUR PAINTING.

French Romantic School   A school of painting of the early 19th cent led by Eugene Delacroix which developed (rather than revolted against) the *Neo-Classical School* (q.v.).   The term "Romantic" applied to the school refers to the treatment and the attitude of the artist rather than to the subject matter of the paintings; for the works of both schools were highly romantic in theme.   The school was expressive of the revolutionary spirit of the time and sought inspiration in the discoveries of natural science and the theories of political philosophy.   It experimented with realism on the one hand (Courbet) and fantasy on the other, and also with the "back

53

to nature" impulse which in its turn gave rise to *Impressionism* (q.v.). The treatment of the Romantics is exemplified by the development of three-dimensional lighting by Gericault and the use of looser drawing by Delacroix.

Fresco The more usual method of mural decoration in Europe, true fresco (or Buon Fresco) is a method of painting on plaster while it is still wet, which requires that no more of the final coat of thin plaster, or *intonaco*, must be applied to the wall to be decorated than the artist can cover in one day. This method ensures that the pigment is completely amalgamated with the plaster, and is therefore permanent, but this is only true in the driest of climates. *Fresco secco* is a method in which the pigments, mixed with lime water, are applied to the plaster after it has dried.

Frontality, Law of In archaic Greek sculpture through most of the 6th cent. B.C. the statue was always conceived from the directly frontal aspect in such a fashion that a vertical line drawn through the nose and navel would, except in the disposition of the limbs, divide it symmetrically. This is known as the Law of Frontality.

Frottage (Fr. a rubbing, the act of rubbing) A technique originated by the Surrealist, Max Ernst, whereby an uneven surface is transferred to paper by rubbing with charcoal or similar substance as in brass-rubbing. The purpose is usually to stimulate the imagination of the artist by suggesting shapes and designs, though the actual frottage itself is sometimes embodied in a composition.

Fugitive Colours Pigments which are easily affected by the action of atmosphere, sunlight and moisture, and which, if used in painting, will cause the picture to fade, darken or otherwise change until the artist's original intention is completely lost. Pigments of animal or vegetable origin (organic pigments) are on the whole untrustworthy, and those most hopelessly fugitive are now rendered obsolete by the manufacture of synthetic pigments of equivalent colour value.

Functionalism   From about 1924, the French architect Le Corbusier (formerly Pierre Jeanneret) began to apply the austere principles of the Purist Movement in painting (See PURISM) to architecture and furnishing, designing in the materials of concrete, steel and glass for purely functional purposes ". . . the house a machine for living in". The style was in vogue between the two wars, and although its severity has been largely modified in recent years, the style remains the basis of most modern architecture.

Futurism   An Italian doctrine in painting and literature which sought to express the violence of the early 20th cent. and the glorification of war and the machine. The first manifesto of the movement was published in 1909 by the writer Marinetti, but it was not until 1911 that the first examples of painting and sculpture appeared by the Futurist artists Severini, Balla and Boccioni. Futurist painting derived from Cubist principles and the bright colour of the Post-Impressionists, but its distinctive feature was the attempt to express rapid movement by the principle of *simultaneity* (q.v.).

G

Galbe   The outline or silhouette of an article of pottery seen in elevation.

Gallery Varnish   A varnish used by the National Gallery during the period 1824-53 composed of mastic dissolved in turpentine. The tendency of all varnishes to darken in time is particularly notice-able in the case of Gallery Varnish, and its use was discontinued after its condemnation by the Select

5

Committee on the National Gallery of 1853. But it remained on many important works until the 1947 cleaning.

Gandhara Art   See GRAECO-BUDDHIST ART.

Ganosis   A process of toning down the glare of marble in sculpture.

Genre   Paintings are sometimes classified according to subject into various groups or "genres" such as landscape, portrait, still-life, historical etc. The term is more commonly used, however, to describe paintings of familiar, everyday life (Brueghel, de Hooch, Hogarth). Sometimes "genre" is used when speaking of the characteristic peculiar to a particular artist.

Geometric Art   A' phrase used to describe that style of art where an object is distorted in representation in the interests of design. The style recurs frequently in the history of art mainly in the northern cultures such as Scandinavian, Saxon, Celtic, Scythian, Early Greek and Byzantine, and it emphasises the rhythmical content of natural forms at the expense, to a greater or lesser degree, of natural appearances. The geometric style is the style of early Greek Sculpture, Celtic manuscript illumination and Byzantine mosaics. Dr. Herbert Read sees in the production of Geometric Art a fundamental attitude in all artistic activity with which he contrasts *organic art* (q.v.).

German Expressionism   See EXPRESSIONISM and DIE BRÜCKE.

Gesso (It.)   A paste-like material compounded of Plaster of Paris or chalk and glue, used as a *ground* (q.v.) in painting. *Gesso Grosso* is a coarse gesso prepared with unslaked plaster and used for the first undercoat. *Gesso Sottile* is a fine gesso prepared from slaked plaster and used for the final surface coat. *Gesso Duro* is a harder variety of gesso.

Gestalt (Ger. form, shape)   A theory originated by the German psychologist C. v. Ehrenfels to describe an object of perception which is incapable of expression simply in terms of its parts. A painting, for example, has aesthetic significance where contemplation of its individual elements would be meaningless.

Ghent School   A school of miniature painters which included the famous families of miniaturists, the Binninks and the Horenbauts, centred in Ghent during the 15th cent.

Glaze (Cer.)   Silicates used for decoration of pottery and protection against moisture. After application the pot is fired and the glaze melts into a glassy covering.

Glazing   A term used in painting to describe the laying of a transparent and comparatively dark colour over a lighter colour so that the underlying colour shows through.

Glory   The representation in painting of opened heavens displaying celestial persons or paradise.

Glyptic Arts   Those arts concerned with carving, particularly the carving of gems.

Gobelin   The name of a celebrated French family of tapestry makers who established themselves at Faubourg St. Marcel on the Bièvre about the middle of the 15th cent. and who are flourishing to this day.

Godescalc, School of   A Carolingian school of illuminators and miniature painters named after the writer Godescalc who, between 781 and 783, wrote an Evangeliar for Charlemagne.

Golden Section   If a given line is cut so that the shorter part is in the same ratio to the longer as the longer is to the whole, then the line is divided by the "Golden Section" or "Golden Mean", a harmonious proportion which has concerned philosophers of art since the earliest days of Greek

philosophy.   Analysis of many works of art will
certainly show that the main lines of the composition
divide the area, or cut the frame, in this proportion:
but whether the artist concerned has adopted it
deliberately or achieved it intuitively is not always
known. The German writer Zeising claimed that
the section existed in all works of art and also in
the structure of natural forms, a claim, however, that
experiment has not upheld.

Gothic   Gothic is used foremostly to describe the
type of architecture, distinguished by its high and
sharply pointed arches and clustered columns, which
appeared in France at the beginning of the 12th cent.
But the word describes not only the type of architecture, but the spirit which produced it, a spirit
that was a strange blending of earthy exuberance
and pious, aspiring devotion.   The great Gothic
cathedrals which arose all over Europe from the 12th
to the 15th cents. were produced by people inspired
by a living sense of religion (perhaps the result of
the humanitarian teachings of St. Francis) who were
at the same time possessed by a childlike visual
curiosity and an enormous sensuous gusto.   The old,
stiff Romanesque style was remoulded to express in
soaring arches and vaulted roofs the lofty religious
aspirations of the builders, while a multitude of
profane details, stained glass portraying temporal
themes such as the seasons, labour and commerce,
grotesque carvings, frequently humorous and sometimes bordering on the obscene, expressed the irre-
pressible humanity of the generations of craftsmen
and labourers who worked on the building.

But the full flavour of the Gothic spirit is found
at its best in the profusion of illuminated manuscripts which were poured out from the monasteries
in the 13th and 14th cents.   In these psalters, missals
and Books of Hours, the grotesque, humorous or
macabre whims of hundreds of anonymous Gothic
artists were allowed full rein, and were expressed in

58

a wealth of intricate design, imaginative illustration and fanciful landscape. From the study of these elaborate and exquisitely produced miniatures one comes to appreciate fully the astonishing enthusiasm and verve for the world of the senses, together with a genuine regard for the spiritual life that was the essence of the Gothic spirit.

Gouache A method of watercolour painting in which the pigments are mixed with white and used opaquely. This is the ancient method of painting in watercolour which was superseded for a long time by the transparent method. Gouache has been revived in recent years and is being used extensively by artists of the Modern British School, Piper, Sutherland, Burra etc.

Graeco-Buddhist Art A name applied to a school of sculpture which existed in Gandhara (North West India and Afghanistan) from the 1st to the 6th cents. A.D. on the assumption that a school of Hellenistic art there was responsible for the unmistakable, though debased, Classic tendencies in Asiatic art. This theory, however, is without conclusive evidence, and from the date and style of the Gandhara monuments it would seem that the sculpture is more likely that of a minor Roman provincial school.

Graeco-Roman Art Name given to early Roman art when it was strongly influenced by Greek culture and of which it is often regarded as being the degenerate continuation.

Graffito (It. graffio, a scratch) Properly, a method of decorating pottery by scratching through an overglaze to reveal a different coloured ground. The technique is also used in painting where one coat of paint is scratched away to reveal an underlying coat of different colour.

Grand Manner, The   A painting in The Grand Manner is one conceived on a large scale with a noble theme and executed in a grandiose style.

Graphic Arts   Used to describe those arts which are concerned with the use of any method of drawing such as pen, pencil, graver, etching needle or brush.

Greek Art   Our knowledge of prehistoric Greek art is derived mainly from extant examples of vase painting which expressed, even from earliest times, the objective attitude to the universe characteristic of all Greek art. At first these vases were decorated by severe geometric designs which were subservient to the primary concern with the forms of the vases themselves, but later the decoration became less subordinate and more naturalistic, using motifs based on animals and plants. The end of this prehistoric period saw the rise in importance of monumental stone sculpture which, during the archaic period (600-500 B.C.) became the leading form of artistic expression. (See ARCHAIC GREEK SCULPTURE). Vase painting during the Archaic period became increasingly naturalistic, illustrating mythological scenes and later scenes of social events, sports, dances, feasts etc. (See BLACK FIGURED VASES & RED FIGURED VASES.

The art of Classical Greece in its most characteristic form was broadly based upon two general concepts (1) The representation of the healthy human form at its best engaged in normal human activity with a tendency towards the heroic (in sculpture, e.g. the Parthenon Frieze and the statues of Myron, Phidias, Praxiteles etc.). (2) A strong sense of formal design. The effect in most cases was an appeal to the intellect rather than to the senses.

But it is in architecture that the Greek genius for order and proportion is best expressed, and comparison of the three orders (Doric, Ionic and

Corinthian) with the later elaborated versions of the Romans demonstrates its noble simplicity and restrained beauty.

Greek Canon   A division of the human body into mathematical proportions, i.e. the total height of the body should ideally be equal to that of eight heads.   There were various canons in early Greek sculpture, but Polyclitus of Argos (450-420) was the first to formulate an exact system which Vitruvius reconstructed with the palm of the hand as unit.

Grisaille   Painting in grey monochrome.   Also an effect of light and shade produced in enamel ware by blending the required tones into a background of opaque white.

Grotesque   A form of decorative painting or sculpture in which human or animal forms are interwoven with flowers and foliage.

Ground   The initial covering on a canvas or support of paint, gesso or glue which renders it suitable to receive the pigments of which the painting is to consist.   The ground will protect the support against dampness and chemical action of the atmosphere and will produce a surface pleasing to work upon.

Gupta Period (320 - 600 A.D.).   A period often known as the Golden Age of Indian civilization, exemplified by the wall paintings of the Ajanta sanctuaries and the statues at Muttra.   In both cases, although the gestures and positions are determined by Buddhist convention, the figures are presented with grace and grandeur, and with the combination of spiritual and sensual beauty which is a feature of all Indian art.

Gustavian Style   Swedish art of the 18th cent. inspired by the Louis XVIth style of France, and executed largely by imported artists and craftsmen.

H

Haarlem School   A 16th cent. school of Dutch painters whose chief characteristic was the truthful representation of garden backgrounds in their paintings, an idea first introduced by Dirk Bouts in the previous century.

Half Length   A standard size of canvas (40" × 50"), used for portraits which included the bust.

Halmstadgruppen   A contemporary group of painters working along Surrealist lines, centred in Halland in Sweden. Artists associated with the group are Axel Olsen, Stellan Mörner and Sven Jonson.

Han Art   This is the art of the Han Dynasty in China (206 B.C. to 220 A.D.), a period that would appear to be in many ways one of great importance in the history of the development of Chinese Art from the primitive. In both painting and sculpture, for example, while the techniques employed were still primitive, there existed an ability to grasp and portray the movement and gesture of living forms. The period is notable for the first use of paper and silk in painting and for the use of glazes in pottery. During the reign of Yaun-Ti (48 - 33 B.C.) an artist, Mao-Yen-Shou, is the first mentioned by name.

Hare's Fur Glaze   A radiating glaze found on some specimens of Sung pottery.

Harmonic Colour   See COLOUR.

Hatching   In drawing, a method of representing tone by lines of varying thickness drawn close together. Cross hatching is a method of lowering the tone still more by hatching one set of lines over another at an angle.

Head Size   A standard size of canvas (20" × 24"), for small portraits of the head only.

Helladic Art   One of the mainland phases of Pre-Hellenic art in the Aegean basin.

Hellenic Art   See GREEK ART.

Hellenistic Art   The name given to the art of Greece during the period of geographical expansion (300-100 B.C.). · Hellenistic art was produced in Asia Minor and in the Aegean Islands and is considerably lacking in the vitality which is characteristic of original Greek art.

Heraldic Colour   See COLOUR.

Heroic Realism   The artistic principle of the Artists' Association of Revolutionary Russia, *Akkhr* (q.v.), which, like the *Wanderers Movement* (q.v.), was moral and literary in tendency and aimed at mass appeal through a realistic style.

Hieratic Art   A conventional type of art, based on earlier forms and traditions and used exclusively for religious purposes, as in the art of ancient Egypt where the majority of art still surviving is of this kind, although there is sufficient evidence to show that a more popular, humanistic art existed at the same time.

High Light   In naturalistic or realistic painting, the areas of highest tonal value, usually representative of the reflection of sunlight (or artificial light if that be the source of illumination) on a surface. See TONE.

High Renaissance   The period, roughly the early 16th cent. when the art of the Italian Renaissance reached its zenith in the work of the great Italian masters.   Leonardo da Vinci (1452 - 1519), Michelangelo (1475-1564). Correggio (1494-1534), Giorgione (1477-1510), Titian (1477-1576), Veronese (1528-1583), Tintoretto (1518-94).

Historiated   Decorated with living forms (human figures, animals, flowers) as distinct from non-representative design such as scrollwork etc.

Hobbyists   See DADA.

Hohenstaufen Art   German art of the Hohenstaufen Dynasty (1138-1254). This period of German art, because of its humanistic interest and tendency towards rationalization has been called the Proto-Renaissance, or the forerunner of the Renaissance.

Hudson River School   A native American school started by the painter Thomas Cole in 1825 which was principally concerned with landscape.

Humanistic Art   Art which is free from the restraint of a dynastic or religious control where the artist is at liberty to give an interpretation of life which is in accordance with his own experience. The great period of Humanistic Art was the period of the Renaissance when, under the liberating influence of the new Greek learning, men's minds were freed from narrow religious preoccupations and artists were turned to temporal themes for inspiration.

Husfield School (Norwegian, Homecraft School)   A Norwegian centre for the study of domestic science, handicrafts and applied arts.

I   J

I.C.A. (**Institute of Contemporary Arts**)   A recent organisation founded by a committee of eminent artists and critics under the chairmanship of Dr. Herbert Read, to "Co-ordinate the arts of our time and establish a common ground for a progressive movement". The Institute aims at stimulating painting, sculpture, music, literature, ballet, theatre, architecture, films and radio, and has so far produced two valuable exhibitions, "Forty Years of Modern Art" and "40,000 Years of Modern Art".

Icon or Ikon (Gr. Image, likeness)   A representation of a sacred personage, executed either in paint, low-relief or mosaic, used extensively in the Greek Orthodox Church. The picture is often encased in metal to represent figure and drapery, leaving the face and hands revealed.

Iconography   The art of representing by images and figures. Also the study of the art.

Idealism   When this term is used in art, it bears two interpretations. (1) In a purely aesthetic sense it refers to the theory of abstraction or pure form. (2) The portrayal of noble themes in an idealistic manner, e.g. Classical Greek sculpture.

Il Fronte Nuovo Delle Arti   The most recent concerted movement in art in post-war Italy, founded by artists of the resistance and originally named *Secessione Artistica Italiana*. Fronte Nuovo is largely Communist in origin and includes the painters Renato Guttuso, Renato Birolli, Armando Pizzinato and the sculptor Alberto Viani. The work of these artists is largely abstract and is directly inspired by contemporary French painting.

Illuminating   The art of decorating manuscripts, usually on vellum, in gold and colours, usually red, blue and sometimes green and purple.

Illusionism   In art, the creation as nearly as possible of an appearance of visual reality. Attainment of this ideal has been mainly restricted to such minor arts as waxworks. In the realm of the fine arts few artists, with the possible exception of some of those of the 19th cent., can be said to have attempted it.

Impasto   The layer of paint comprising the surface of a painting, and also the manner of handling it peculiar to an artist. But the expression is more often used to describe the application of paint in a particularly heavy or solid fashion.

Impressionism   Broadly defined, Impressionism in art concerns itself with the recording of the ephemeral "impression" of a scene. Impressionist artists in this sense include Whistler, Sargent, Constable (in his sketches), Turner and even Rembrandt.

65

The term applies specifically, however, to a particular movement which came into being during the late 19th cent. in France and which, although intended as the final stage in the rendering of natural appearances, became the forerunner, and in fact the basis of, the revolutionary movements which were to follow in defiance of the accepted laws of vision.

The Impressionists were inspired by a scientific study of light, and in order to represent appearances more accurately, introduced the *Spectrum Palette*. (q.v.). This was composed of pure bright colours, corresponding to the spectrum of sunlight, which were applied to the canvas without previously mixing on the palette. Bright sunlight was rendered in a series of bright yellows, and shadows were seen as deep violet. The leaders of the movement, which was also known as *Luminism*, were Monet, Sisley, and Pissarro; and other painters who, while not subscribing to the principles, adopted the technique were Renoir, Degas, Manet, and the early *Post-Impressionists* (q.v.) Cézanne, Van Gogh, Gauguin and the *Neo-Impressionists* (q.v.).

Indian Art   All Indian art has been inspired by and dedicated to various religions, Buddhism, Hinduism, Jainism, and for this reason, despite their great beauty, all Indian monuments are utilitarian in concept. Beauty, in fact, is incidental and not a conscious purpose of the artist who has not been concerned with creation for its own sake. See GRAECO-BUDDHIST ART; GUPTA PERIOD; MOGHUL ART; RAJPUT PAINTING.

Indo-Sumerian   A term sometimes used to describe the *Indus Valley Art* (q.v.).

Induced Colour   The tendency of a colour to appear complementary to that of the main or predominant object in a scene or picture. Thus a red apple appears redder when standing on a green cloth, but would take on a violet or crimson hue

66

were the ground yellow. In the same way a blue ground would make the apple appear orange.

Indus Valley Art   The art of the Indus Valley civilization provides the earliest known examples of art in India.   Fragments of sculpture have been found in the ancient city of Mohenjo Daro which flourished from around 3000 B.C. to 2000 B.C.   But much more numerous are the small seals portraying in very life-like form typically Indian animals such as the elephant, ox and zebu, as well as representations of Indian and Mesopotamian deities.   Articles of Indian manufacture have also been found in certain centres of early Babylonian culture from which it is assumed that there was a certain artistic link between the two civilizations.   Thus the term Indo-Sumerian has sometimes been used to describe the art of Mohenjo Daro.

Inert   Any material, such as chalk and china clay, which is used for giving body to a pigment in painting.

Intaglio (It. engraving, engraved work)   A form of gem or seal engraving where the design is incised into the stone so as to appear in relief when the seal is pressed into hot wax.

Intarsia   A method of producing designs by inlaying wood in a background of wood.

Integral Vision   A phrase used by Dr. Herbert Read to describe the principle of composition used by Henri Matisse.   Dr. Read points out that Matisse developed his composition round a central focus point, and while the eye of the spectator is on this focus point the rest of the picture falls into place, but when the eye is removed from this point and the work examined analytically, the parts of the picture appear meaninglessly distorted.

Intimistes   The name of a small school of French painters headed by Pierre Bonnard and Edouard Vuillard, who stood aside from the turbulence of late

19th cent. invention and experimentation, and quietly developed their own form of *Impressionism* (q.v.). The name arises from their portrayal of local and cosily intimate themes.

Intonaco In fresco painting, the final coat of fine quality plaster applied to the wall to receive the painting.

Inv. Abbreviation of Invenit (Latin 'he invented'). Found on engravings to indicate by whom the original was designed.

Isocephaly A style of composition, characteristic of the Classical period of Greek art, in which figures in a composition are arranged so that they are of the same height.

Italianizers The name of a group of Flemish painters of the 16th and 17th cents. which included Mabuse and Jan Masys, who developed a native style which was a blend of Italian and Flemish painting.

Jack of Diamonds Group, The A group of Russian painters, one of the *Russian Futurist* movements, and later incorporated in the *Akkhr* (q.v.), formed round the first Russian followers of Cézanne in 1910.

Japanese Prints A traditional form of Japanese popular art, produced in multiple colour from wood blocks (See WOODCUT), a process in which their skill has seldom been rivalled. These prints have had considerable influence on western art and were a source of inspiration to such painters as Whistler, Van Gogh and Toulouse-Lautrec.

Jugendstil The German equivalent of *Art Nouveau* (q.v.), the name being derived from the magazine "Jugend" first published in Munich in 1896.

K

Kakemono (Jap.) A Japanese or Chinese hanging painting usually mounted on cloth for wall decoration.

Kamares Ware   See AEGEAN VASES.

K'ang-Hsi Ware   This porcelain, produced during
the dynasty of that name (1662-1722 A.D.) is
regarded as the finest in the history of Chinese
ceramics in its decorative aspect. It incorporates
etched and embossed designs and unusual glaze
effects imitative of jade, metals and marble.

Kaolin (Chinese 'High Ridge' referring to place where
the clay was originally found)   The original
white China clay used in the manufacture of *porcelain*
(q.v.). Kaolin is a decayed felspar rock, and is
non-fusible (or refractory) and requires the addition
of a fusing agent which in the original Chinese
porcelain is *Petuntse* (q.v.).

Kinetic Sculpture (Moving Sculpture)   A development of *Equipoised Sculpture* (q.v.) first used by the
Constructivists (Gabo, Moholy-Nagy, Pevsner) which
set out to express the relationships of volumes in
movement. The material (usually thin bodies such
as wire, rings etc.) was used not as a mass, but as a
vehicle for movement, in fact it was ideally intended
to be transformed into "a kind of ethereal extension
appearing without mass or heaviness". It was "a
weightless poising of volumes, relationships and inter-
penetrations".

The American sculptor, Alexander Calder, has
made kinetic constructions of balls and bent wires
which he calls *mobiles* (q.v.) or "plastic forms in
motion". In an article in *Horizon*, October 1941,
the painter Ben Nicholson refers to his first encounter
with one of these mobiles, "a large black, five small
white, and one small scarlet, balls on thin wires"
turning slowly in the breeze "with their shadows
chasing round the white walls in an exciting inter-
changing movement".

Kit-Kat   A size of canvas (28″ × 36″) used for
portraits of less than half length but including the
hands. The size was used for portraits of members

69

of the famous Kit-Kat Club, whose dining room was too low to allow half-length portraits.

Kouri & Kourai   See Archaic Greek Sculpture.

L

Lacquer   A painting medium, obtained from the sap of the sumac tree, which gives a hard and lasting surface with a great intrinsic beauty. It is in this respect a method of painting peculiar to the Orient, but synthetic cellulose products exhibiting similar qualities are being used experimentally in Europe in the fine arts.

Lapis Lazuli   A semi-precious stone used as a medium for carving. The powdered stone is the source of the pigment ultramarine in its genuine form but has now been almost completely replaced by various artificial products. Nothing can equal the quality of the true pigment, however, the beauty of which can be seen in illuminated manuscripts.

L'Art Rupestre (Fr. from the Latin Rupas, a rock) A' phrase used to cover all those types of art which are engraved or drawn on rocks or in caves by primitive races of men.

La Tène Art   A style of Celtic art of the 1st cent. B.C. which derives its name from the site in France where the best known objects of this style were found (See Celtic Art).

Lattice   A form of ornament in which diagonal lines cross each other at regular intervals to form diamond shaped spaces.

Lay Figure   A jointed wooden model of the human figure used by artists as a model for poses or for the arrangement of costume, draperies etc.

Light and Shade   By the use of light and shade (the representation of illumination) the artist gives volume to his shapes and is able to give an effect of three-dimensional space in his picture. See TONE.

Line Since line as such does not exist in nature, its use in representative art can only symbolize reality, and this the draughtsman achieves by various devices such as varying the thickness of lines in order to suggest recession, projection and the interrelation of planes. Line, however, possesses a rhythmic vitality of its own without reference to any form that it may be concerned with representing, and it is this "dancing" quality which is the mark of the master draughtsman, and provides the interest in works of a purely abstract nature.

Line & Wash A method of drawing in monochrome or coloured wash in which the outline of the more important forms are delineated with pen or brush in black or sepia ink.

Line Engraving The original method of *engraving* (q.v.) in which a graver or burin is used to incise lines on a steel plate, the hardness of which material enforces a certain angularity to the line, wherein lies the characteristic feature of the method. No use of the burr is made, as in drypoint, and a large printing is therefore possible, hence its use as a method of book illustration in the 17th and 18th cents. until superseded by wood engraving and eventually process engraving. It is still practised as an art form by modern print makers.

Literary Art This expression is generally used to describe the kind of painting which tells a story or illustrates an incident as in Hogarth's "Rake's Progress" series or Millais' "Order of Release". This narrative form, however, is only one aspect of literary art which can also be used to describe works which have a poetic content or atmosphere as in the work of such modern painters as Paul Nash ("Pillar & Moon") and John Piper (drawings of Knole). It seems to be a fact that this literary quality is a peculiarly distinctive characteristic of most English painting in contrast to the formal and intellectual preoccupations of continental schools. See NEO-ROMANTICISM.

Lithography   A method of reproducing a drawing which depends upon the antipathy of grease and water. The drawing is made on a lithographic stone or steel plate, with a greasy crayon, ink or paint. The stone being then saturated with water, the printing ink is applied and adheres only to those portions covered by the crayon etc. A separate drawing is required for each colour contained in the print.

Local Colour   The apparently natural colour of an object which, when represented in a painting, is usually modified by the effects of light and shade and *reflected* or *induced colour* (qq.v.).

London Group   At the beginning of the present century the *Camden Town Group* (q.v.) absorbed the more advanced and independent currents in the art of the day to become *The London Group* under the first Presidency of Harold Gilman. Amongst its original members it numbered Walter Sickert, Spencer Gore, Charles Ginner and the Vorticist painter Wyndham Lewis. The London Group took over from the New English Art Club as the centre of progressive art in England, a function which it still performs with a wide and varied membership which includes Lawrence Gowing, Duncan Grant, Ivon Hitchens, Henry Moore, Victor Passmore, Ceri Richards, William Roberts, Matthew Smith, Ruskin Spear and John Tunnard. Until their deaths, both Paul Nash and Mark Gertler were members.

Louvain School   A school of 15th cent Flemish artists centred in Louvain and headed by Dirk Bouts.

Luminists   An alternative name for the French Impressionists of the late 19th cent. See IMPRESSION-ISM. Also applied to a group of American 19th cent.

painters who developed the Impressionist theories in the U.S.A.

Lumia   An experimental fine art form in which colour compositions are produced by the manipulation of a range of coloured lights. The first successful experiment was a colour organ constructed by Professor Rimington in which a screen was flushed with varying colours from lamps controlled by an organ keyboard. In his book *Colour Music*, published in 1912, Professor Rimington endeavoured to show the relationship of colour to music and in his experiments he "played" colour sonatas.

M

Macchinisti   A group of Italian painters of the late 16th cent. who adopted an exaggerated and over-colourful style.

Magdalenian Art   See PREHISTORIC ART.

Magischer Realismus (Ger. Magic Realism)   An alternative name for *Die Neue Sachlichkeit* (q.v.).

Magot (Fr.)   A name contemptuously applied to certain grotesque figures in porcelain or ivory produced in China and Japan to meet the uncritical 19th cent. European taste for 'chinoiserie.'

Maitres Populaires   French name for *Sunday Painters* (q.v.).

Majolica   A species of fine Italian pottery in which the article is coated with tin enamel and the decoration painted on and then fired. The name is also applied to ware similarly produced in other countries.

Makimono (Jap.)   A Japanese or Chinese scroll painting wound on rollers (See CHINESE ART).

Malerische   A German word for "painterly values" which are the purely technical and objective values of the artist as distinct from the aesthetic or psychological values of the painting as a work of art.

Mannerism   The distinctive characteristic of an artist's style (in particular an emphasis on technical dexterity) which he exploits to cover the absence of original creativity in his work.

Mannerist Style   A term applied to a style of art which flourished at the time of the Late Renaissance, i.e. from about 1520 to 1600, from the end of the High Renaissance to the beginning of the Baroque period. The style, which was symptomatic of the exhaustion of the original creative impulse of the Renaissance, expressed itself by a looseness of composition and exaggerated and insignificant gesture as exemplified by the work of Cavaliere d'Arpino and the *Eclectics* (q.v.) and the *Chiaroscurists* (q.v.).

Maquette   A rough miniature model used by the sculptor as a guide to the large complete work.

Marouflage (Fr.)   A method of protecting canvases by gluing them to a wall or panel.

Marquetry (Fr. marqueter, to inlay)   The art of inlaying wood with other woods of varying colours, or with other materials such as tortoise-shell, ivory, metal or mother-of-pearl. Marquetry was particularly fashionable for decorating furniture in the 19th cent.

Mass   In painting, mass refers to any large form or group of forms or to any large area of colour, light or shade. It constitutes the positive element in a work of art in contrast to the negative one of space. Thus, mass and space are complementary, the one being the inversion of the other. The successful contrasting of masses is an important element in the composition of a picture.

Matière (Fr.)   An expression used when referring to the intrinsic qualities of the surface of a painting.

Maulstick (sometimes MAHLSTICK)   A light stick with a leather-padded tip used by the painter as a support for his brush hand.

Mecanomorphic Fetishes In Surrealistic art, particularly that of Marcel Duchamp, the expression of an obsession with machine forms and mechanical functions, which even sees the internal workings of the human body as a mechanical contrivance.

Medium By medium is meant the material means with which the artist gives shape to his artistic conception. The peculiar characteristics of each of the various media are so fundamental a part of a work of art that the artist will usually have the medium to be used in view when the idea is conceived, and certainly will bear the limitations of his medium in mind when executing the work. No painter would use oils, for example, to render an effect more naturally obtained by water-colour, nor would a sculptor attempt, while modelling in clay, to give his work qualities characteristic of carved stone.

The more usual media used in painting are: oils, tempera, distemper, fresco, wax-painting and mosaic; and in drawing: lead pencil, ink, crayon, pastel and charcoal, and various combined methods such as line and wash. Sculpture is modelled in clay and some-times in wax (usually for reproduction by casting in metal) or carved directly in stone, wood or ivory. There are also the arts of steel and copper engraving, etching, drypoint, mezzotint, aquatint, wood en-graving, woodcut, lithography, and the crafts of pottery, weaving etc.

In a more technical sense, medium refers to the liquid, such as water, turpentine, etc., which is used in painting to render the pigment fluid and workable.

Megilp In oil painting, a mixture of mastic varnish and pale drying oil. Other compound media are sometimes called megilp and the term is also used in gouache and watercolour painting to describe a preparation mixed with the colour to prevent rapid drying or to render its application easier.

Melanesian Art See OCEANIC PRIMITIVE ART.

Meldrum, School of The name of a group of Australian painters inspired by the teachings of the painter Duncan Max Meldrum who founded the Meldrum Art School in Melbourne in 1913. Meldrum's principles are "that painting is a pure science" and that the task of a painter is to translate visual impressions in terms of tone, proportion and colour in that order of importance. Max Meldrum has expounded his theories in his book *The Invariable Truths of Depictive Art*, 1917.

Metz, School of A Carolingian school of illuminators and miniature painters at the beginning of the 9th century.

Mezzo-Relievo (It.) Middle relief in sculpture, now classified by modern usage with low-relief.

Mezzotint An engraving process which bears some resemblance to the *drypoint* process (q.v.) in that it produces the same deep velvety tones by means of a burr. In this case, however, the burr is first produced by roughening the whole surface of the plate (usually by means of a many-toothed tool called a 'rocker') which if printed would give a solid black. The artist then produces his design by scraping away the burr to print lighter tones where required, the tone varying according to the depth of the scraping, a pure white resulting where the original smooth surface of the copper is revealed.

Ming The last great age in Chinese art was that of the Ming Dynasty (1368-1644 A.D.) which derived inspiration from the much earlier *T'ang* Dynasty (q.v.) whose spirit it managed to capture to some extent without achieving the same high standard. The great achievements of Ming art were in the sphere of ceramics. In 1369, large Imperial kilns were established, and under the patronage of successive emperors porcelain technique was perfected in a style based largely on *Sung* (q.v.) models but substituting polychromatic finishes for the simple and elegant monochrome of that style. Rich colours were used (turquoise blue and violet, and a green interior glaze) and the *cloisonné* process (q.v.) was used to separate the coloured glazes.

Miniature Painting   The word 'miniature' originally applied to the small illustrations in illuminated manuscripts and later to the large initial letters with their pictorial embellishments.   In more recent times the word has been more exclusively applied to small portrait painting on ivory or enamel.   Ivory is the most commonly used ground for this form of painting as its natural tint assists in producing flesh colouring. Miniature painting has a long tradition in this country, the most outstanding artists being Nicholas Hilliard (1537 - 1619), Isaac Oliver (1556 - 1617), Richard Cosway (1742-1821) and Sir William Ross (1794-1860). The last executed over 2,000 miniatures. Although the age of the miniature has long been over, the tradition is still maintained by a small band of amateur devotees.

Minoan Art   See CRETAN-MINOAN.

Missal   The Prayer Book of the Roman Catholic Church, containing the service for the Mass through-out the year, which has provided an opportunity for much fine work in the art of illumination.

Mobiles   See KINETIC SCULPTURE.

Modelling   (1) Modelling is that division of sculpture in which the figure is formed in some malleable material, usually clay but sometimes wax, either to be retained as the finished work of art or, as is most usual, to be cast in metal such as bronze or lead.

(2) In painting and drawing, modelling is the process, by the use of light and shade, whereby a third-dimensional effect is achieved.

Modern Classical Renaissance   A term used by the critic R. H. Wilenski to describe the revolt against Impressionism which took place during the years 1884 to 1891. The artists concerned included Seurat, Renoir, Cézanne, Degas and Toulouse-Lautrec who, while continuing to use the Impressionist colour theory, were more concerned with painting pictures of a formal nature. The Modern Classical Revival was a trend rather than a movement among a group of highly individualistic painters, and through Cézanne paved the way for *Post-Impressionism* (q.v.).

Moderner Bund A group of Swiss artists, organised by the French sculptor, Jean Arp, during his stay in Weggis in Switzerland during the years 1908-9. The group was short-lived and contributed towards the freeing of art from the merely imitative.

Moghul Art The Art of the Mohammedan emperors of India during the 16th and 17th centuries A.D. Painting was mainly concerned with the production of manuscripts and isolated album miniatures, executed with a delicacy and a feeling for detail inspired by the Persian founders of the 'school' and the native Indian lavishness of colour. The Moghul style in architecture, of which the Taj Mahal is probably the best known example, is characterised by slender columns, heavily domed roofs and marble grills.

Mohammedan Art Mohammedan Art makes no distinction between the fine and useful arts, and the Moslems have never regarded the artist as a person from whom to expect spiritual insight. They classify painting among such crafts as weaving and ceramics and even in its finest form merely as an adjunct to book production, while architecture, except in its theoretical aspect, is often the work of the master mason. Calligraphy is the sole exception, being regarded as "a spiritual geometry", and has been enthusiastically practised by scholars and even royalty for its own sake.

Monochrome　　　The art of painting in one colour (usually black or dark brown) and white, so that the tonal nature only of the subject is portrayed.

Monotype　　　A method of taking copies of a painting or drawing made originally on a sheet of glass or other non-absorbant surface with slow-drying paint. The image is transferred by laying the paper on the plate and applying pressure by rubbing. Several copies may be taken but in each case the plate must be to a certain extent repainted, with a resultant variation in colour and design in each print which is therefore unique.

Montage　　　A form of *collage* (q.v.) in which arrangements are made of sections of photographs. This is a strict definition, but the two terms *montage* and *collage*, and to some extent the processes, are sometimes used interchangeably.

Morbidezza　　　An Italian expression for the life-like representation of delicate and soft flesh tints.

Mordant　　　(1) In etching, the acid used to bite in the line on the plate.
　　　　　(2) In gilding, the adhesive film used for fixing the gold leaf.

Mosaic　　　A method of decoration executed by inlaying cubes of coloured stone, metal, glass or enamel on a ground of stucco or mastic. In Roman times the method was used to decorate pavements, but it is more usually associated with Early Christian Art, and it is the recognised form of mural decoration in Byzantine Architecture, particularly in the churches at Ravenna.

　　Aesthetically, mosaic is pre-eminently a satis-factory form of mural, in that the materials used compose part of the actual fabric of the wall, and are not superimposed as is the ease in methods embodying the use of pigments.

Moscow, School of　　　This school of Russian religious art would appear to have been founded by the Master Andrei Rubliov who was also associated with the *School of Novgorod* (q.v.) as in 1405 he collaborated in the decoration of the Church of the Virgin Annunciate in Moscow. The mature style of the school during the 16th century amalgamated elements of the original folk art with Byzantine influences. The sack of Novgorod in 1570 established Moscow as the centre of Russian art, which, however, in this phase lost its distinctive characteristics by the continual absorption of foreign influences from east and west at the expense of its own traditions.

Movement   The terms 'movement' and 'action' are to some extent interchangeable, but movement refers more precisely to the direction of the lines of composition in a picture, while action usually refers to the attitudes or positions of figures and objects in a composition. Thus the outstretched arms of a figure may indicate prayer or supplication, which is the *action* of the figure, but the line made by the arms, linked with other elements in the picture, contributes to the *movement* of the composition.

Multiplacazione (It. multiplication)   A method of composition, most notably used by the contemporary Italian painter Mario Sironi, in which the picture is divided into several compartments each containing a painting related in theme to the whole composition.

Mural Painting   The decoration of walls by painting using such techniques as fresco, oil, tempera, etc., where the painting is made directly onto the wall. An important problem that the painter of a mural often has to face is that of composition within so large a field that the picture cannot be viewed as a whole from any one particular aspect, as in the case of an easel picture. The mural has therefore to be so composed that the portion viewed from any aspect is complete in itself and yet related to the adjoining portions. Similarly, where perspective is employed, the artist may have difficulty in working with the usual one or two vanishing points without apparent distortion in parts not within the immediate field of vision. Some compromise is then necessary to render the scheme convincing as a whole.

N

Nabis, The This group was formed in 1892 by certain painters associated with Gauguin in his Brittany days and inspired by particular aspects of his work. They were closely connected with the *Symbolist* and *Rose-Croix* movements (qq.v.) through their admiration, not only for Gauguin, but also for Puvis de Chavannes. Membership included Maurice Denis, Pierre Bonnard and Edouard Vuillard, although Bonnard and Vuillard, who were later to develop a totally distinct style as the *Intimistes* (q.v.) did not conform with the Symbolist attitude. Toulouse - Lautrec was also associated with the Nabis for a time, as was also Aristide Maillol, not as a sculptor, however, but as a painter.

Narrative Art An extreme form of descriptive or literary art which serves to tell a story or illustrate an incident, as for example, in much late 19th cent. painting in England. The term, although often contemptuously applied, aptly describes many works of considerable artistic merit such as Hogarth's "Marriage à la Mode", the Bayeux Tapestry and certain Egyptian and Babylonian friezes.

Natural Colour See COLOUR.

Naturalism in art aims at achieving a complete resemblance to the object or scene depicted, as opposed to *Realism* (q.v.) which is concerned with revealing the underlying structure. This is not to say, however, that the naturalistic artist is concerned merely with recording a scene with mechanical accuracy or photographic verisimilitude, as a genuine work of art in the naturalistic vein will also convey the artist's feeling for the subject portrayed.

Naturalisti   A school of late 16th cent. Italian painters, founded in Rome by Caravaggio, who set themselves to transcribe nature accurately in opposition to Eclectic Schools. The school also flourished at Naples under the leadership of Polidoro and Sabatini and later included the Spanish painter Ribera during his residence in that city.

Nature Morte   French for *still life* (q.v.).

Nazarenes, The   A name originally applied ironically to a group of early 19th century Viennese artists who revolted from the academic tradition and who took up residence in 1910 in a deserted monastery near Rome and called themselves the Fratelli di San Isidoro. The Nazarenes held that art should primarily serve religious ends, and with this in view they organised themselves into a group which was almost a monastic order, taking as their models the works of the early German and Italian painters, and later the work of Perugino, Raphael and Michelangelo. The movement declined rapidly owing to the fact that they stressed the religious aspects of art to the detriment of the aesthetic and artistic. Furthermore, their romantic spirit was eclipsed by the realistic naturalism of the growing *Biedermeier movement* (q.v.). The leading spirits were the painters Overbeck, Pforr, Hottinger, Wintergerst and Vogel.

Near-Abstract   See ABSTRACT ART.

Negative Carving   A method of carving in stone or wood in which the design is hollowed out of the surface instead of being left in relief. It is specially used for carving matrixes for the casting of medals and coins.

Negro Art refers to the primitive art of the African native in the regions of Yoruba and Benin, the Gold and Ivory Coasts, the Sudan, West Africa and the Congo. The varieties of work produced are extensive, covering wood and stone and ivory carving, clay modelling and metal casting, pottery making and decoration and the lesser domestic arts of basket-making and weaving. Most examples known to us are of comparatively recent origin, but it is agreed that they follow traditions extending back at least as far as the 12th cent. A.D. Apart from the more utilitarian crafts, Negro art is produced for religious purposes and there would seem to be no evidence of art appreciation or criticism in savage societies, which may explain, as Mr. Clive Bell suggests, the failure of such societies to produce great civilizations. There has been, however, no lack of appreciation on the part of Europeans, and there can be no doubt that African Negro Art, along with that of other primitive races, has done more to influence the tendencies of modern European art than traditional historical styles.

Negroism This expression refers to the interest in Negro sculpture cultivated by the Post-Impressionists in France and the Expressionists in Germany, and the influence which it had upon their work particularly in the case of Matisse and the Fauve movement and Picasso in his Negro Period.

Negro Period A short phase in the work of Pablo Picasso lasting roughly from 1907-08, in which he embodied the characteristics of African art into his paintings and sculptures. The best known work of this period is perhaps "Les Desmoiselles d'Avignon".

Neo-Academicism The principle of abstraction has taken so firm a root in modern art, and its use has become so much an idiom with many contemporary painters who have little to offer in the way of originality, that it may be looked upon as the foundation of a new school of academic art against which there may be observed a reaction in favour of a greater degree of representation.

Neo-Classical (Third Reich)　　The superficially classical state-sponsored art style of Nazi Germany, imposed by Hitler to replace the condemned *Degenerate Art* (q.v.).

Neo-Classical School, The　　A French school of painting and sculpture of the late 18th and early 19th cents., the founding of which is usually ascribed to David who revolted against the sensual and romantic art of Watteau and Greuze and the realism of Chardin. Ingres became associated with the school in 1824 after his return from Italy and eventually assumed leadership. Neo-Classical painting was almost decorative in quality, the work of both David and Ingres being more in the nature of draughtsmanship. Other members of the school were Girodet and Prud'hon.

Neo-Gothic　　A style of imitation Gothic architecture introduced into England during the middle of the 19th cent. by the architects Pugin and Barry and encouraged by the writings of John Ruskin. The best examples are the Houses of Parliament and the Law Courts in London. The term is also applied to an earlier phase of interest in the Gothic manifested in the late 18th cent. in connection with the Gothic literary movement of the time, e.g. Horace Walpole's House, Strawberry Hill, at Twickenham.

Neo-Impressionism　　A development of *Impressionism* (q.v.) founded by the French painters Seurat and Signac in the 1880's who devised the method of painting known as *Pointillism* (q.v.) which was not, however, the most important feature of the movement. In contrast with the objectivity of the Impressionists, Seurat and his followers re-introduced a more personal attitude to the subject and stressed the use of line, form and colour. Neo-

Impressionism was, in fact, one of the leading movements which reacted against the 19th cent. naturalism and should properly be regarded as an aspect of *Post-Impressionism* (q.v.).

Neolithic   See PREHISTORIC ART.

Neo-Plasticism   A Dutch movement in abstract art founded in 1920 by Piet Mondriaan, Van Doesburg and Van Tongerloo and associated with the *De Stijl Group* (q.v.). The movement stressed the geometric aspect of Cubism and rejected the representational element which still existed in that movement. Neo-Plasticism, together with *Suprematism* and *Constructivism* (qq.v.) were moving forces in the beginnings of a revolution in architecture and industrial design of which the *Bauhaus* (q.v.) was the outstanding development.

Neo-Primitivism   An alternative name for *Unschooled* and *Sunday Painters* (qq.v.).

Neo-Romanticism   Much of the work of the contemporary British school of painting, although owing a great deal to the influence of the intellectual French experiments of the early years of this cent., has turned once more to the expression of the romantic attitude which is probably the most characteristic aspect of the native tradition. This attitude, which takes the form of a concern with problems of light, feeling and atmosphere and which is sometimes linked with the formal language of the Cubists and Abstractionists and sometimes with the literary preoccupations of the Surrealists, and often with the influences of the 19th cent. Romantics such as Blake, Palmer and Calvert, is generally defined as Neo-Romanticism. The expression is used, not as the title of a specific group or movement, but as a convenient label for a trend or characteristic in the work of such diverse artists as Paul Nash, Graham Sutherland, John Piper, Michael Ayrton, etc.

Neo-Surrealism   See SURREALISM.

Neue Kunstler-vereinigung   See N.K.V.

New English Art Club   Founded in 1886 by English students who wished to develop Impressionist painting in England in revolt against the existing academic traditions. The founders included Wilson Steer and W. R. Sickert who were influenced by the theories of the *Barbizon* and *Impressionist* Schools (qq.v.). These ideas, although still novel in England, were already replaced in Paris by *Post-Impressionism* (q.v.) and certain members of the club soon seceded and developed the newer ideas under the name of *The London Group* (q.v.). The Club, however, continued (and still does to this day) to produce works in the Impressionist tradition, reaching its zenith at the beginning of the century when its membership included such figures as Sir William Orpen, Sir William Rothenstein, Augustus John, Ambrose McEvoy and Lucien Pissarro.

New Objectivity   See DIE NEUE SACHLICHKEIT.

Niello-work   A method of inlaying on metals, usually silver, in which a dark-coloured alloy is used to fill in the engraved design.

Nimbus or Halo   A circle of light surrounding the head of a sacred personage in a painting.

N.K.V.   Abbreviation of *Neue Kunstlervereinigung* German for New Artists' Union, a society formed by Kandinsky and Jawlensky in 1908 after the rejection of some of their work by the German Impressionist society *Sezession* (q.v.). Other members of the society were Adolf Erbsloh, Alexander Kanoldt, Gabriele Munter and Alfred Kubin. Although there was no common ideal amongst the members, their work was influenced by the contemporary French Fauvist, Cubist and Symbolist experiments. The N.K.V. held three exhibitions in Munich in the years 1909, 1910 and 1911, after which differences of opinion caused Kandinsky, Jawlensky, Munter and Kubin to form a new society, the *Blaue Reiter* (q.v.) with a yet more advanced Post-Impressionist outlook.

Nocturne　　　A musical term adopted by J. M. Whistler to describe his paintings of evening and night scenes, and since used generally of any picture of this type.

Non-Figuratif Painting　　　French name for abstract painting.

Non-Objective Painting or Non-Figurative Painting Both these terms are frequently used by critics and writers on art as alternatives for Abstract Painting.

Norman Style (Anglo-Norman)　　　The style of architecture which preceded the Gothic in England and Normandy.　　In England it prevailed mainly during the 12th and early 13th cents. until replaced by the Early English but the style had been in use in France fifty years earlier.　Although the style has many distinctive features of its own, it is usually recognised as the English form of *Romanesque* (q.v.).

Novecento　　　The pretentious, official neo-classical art-style of Fascist Italy.

Novgorod, School of　　　The first manifestations of a truly national art in Russia were centred in Novgorod during the 14th and 15th cents. and it was devoted to religious painting.　"Theophanes the Greek" is the first and most important master mentioned in connection with the school, his work showing an affinity with the Byzantine tradition. The style of the school is marked by an elongation of forms and the use of dramatic highlights and an almost abstract line.　The School was succeeded by that of Moscow as the centre of Russian art during the 16th cent.

Nuremberg, School of　　　A short-lived academy of painting established as a private school of art in Nuremberg by Joachim Nützel in 1662. Under the directorship of Joachim von Sandrart the school was made a public institution, and under his uninspired teaching the academy rapidly declined. None of the students of this academy seems to have risen above a low level of mediocrity.

O

Obelisk   A four-sided monumental figure with a pyramidal top, of which "Cleopatra's Needle" is an example.

Object   A word adopted by the Dadaists and Surrealists for articles, normally found in a non-artistic context, e.g. stones, eggs, sanitary fixtures, garments etc., selected and arranged, singly or in groups, by the artist for aesthetic contemplation.

Object Poem   In Surrealism, the assembly of miscellaneous objects on a panel together with lettering and verse.

Objective Naturalism   A phrase used to describe the school of realist painters led by the French painter Courbet in the middle 19th cent. The recognised title of this school is The Realist Movement, but the term *realist* in this case refers more to the subject matter than to the method of treatment, which is better described as objective-naturalism, i.e. a faithful rendering of the scene in which the artist strives to restrain his personal reactions.

Objets Trouvés   See FOUND OBJECTS.

Oceanic Primitive Art   A general term for the savage art of the South Pacific which includes Australia, Polynesia, Melanesia and Micronesia. The carvings and drawings and other art forms of these areas have aroused interest in recent years largely because of their influence on modern European art, particularly Surrealism as exemplified in Chirico's early work, though much of this primitive work has a high aesthetic interest of its own.

Odalisque   A female slave or concubine in an eastern harem. A popular subject and title with French 19th cent. painters — Renoir, Ingres, Matisse.

Offskip   A somewhat archaic term for the most distant part of a landscape painting.

Oil Painting   A method of painting in which the pigments are ground with oils and diluted with turpentine, oil of spike or refined petrol. The medium is the one most commonly used in painting in Europe since it displaced *tempera* (q.v.) in the 15th cent., and there can be no doubt that its popularity is due to the freedom of its handling and the lack of discipline required compared with tempera, water colour etc. Oil colour is usually applied in various consistencies, from a paste-like stiffness known as *impasto* to a thin transparent *glaze*. Its plasticity is such that it lends itself to many kinds of manipulation and thus permits a range of subtle surface qualities.

Organic Art   A phrase used by Dr. Herbert Read to describe that style of art, produced mainly by southern races, where natural forms are realistically represented. Organic art can be exemplified by the sculpture of Classical Greece where the sole purpose of the artist was the naturalistic rendering of the human form and not distortion for the sake of design as in *geometric art* (q.v.). Dr. Read discusses this subject fully in *The Meaning of Art*.

Original Art   In using this expression, the critic does not mean strange, unfamiliar or abnormal art. The work of an original artist arises from an inner necessity to express an unique point of view, and this is as true of Giotto or Rembrandt as it is of Cézanne or Picasso. (Cf. DERIVATIVE ART).

Ormolu   Gilded brass or bronze used in the decoration of furniture particularly in France in the 18th and early 19th cents.

Ornament   Ornamentation is the embellishment or decoration of the surface of a structure whose essential nature is independent of the added ornament. The study of ornament is of value to the art historian as, since its styles change more frequently than those of the structure which is ornamented, it provides a more exact indication of period.

Ornament is briefly classified as geometrical or naturalistic. Geometric ornament, which tends towards the abstraction of natural forms, is more typical of primitive societies such as the Archaic Greek and savage communities, while the naturalistic variety, which is a frank representation of animal and vegetable motifs, is found in the work of more advanced civilizations such as Classical Greece and Renaissance Italy.

Orphism   See SIMULTANEISME.

Ottonian Art   This period takes its name from the German Emperor Otto the Great of Saxony (936-973 A.D.) but covers the reigns of all the Saxon Kings from 919 to 1024 A.D., and is the first national school of Germany. Ottonian Art developed from the later *Carolingian* style (q.v.) and reached its height and was most fruitful around the year 1000, after which it began the transition to the *Salian* style (q.v.). The period is notable for the foundation of many cathedrals including Mainz, Worms and Essens, and for many fine schools of painting and sculpture of which the most important is the Reichnau School which produced the Egbert Codex commissioned by the brothers Kerald and Heribert. Ottonian Art is also known as Pre- or Early Romanesque.

Outline   "Nature has no outline, but imagination has", said William Blake in order to urge the necessity for good drawing, even in painting. Outline was man's earliest device for recording his visual experiences, and it is only during recent years, with the rise of "painting" by tonal values that it has been dispensed with. With the revolt against the cult of naturalism in painting, however, the outline has been used in modern art with effect as in the work of Gauguin, Matisse, Rouault and others.

Overglaze Painting   In ceramics, the application of decoration after glazing

P

Painterly   A term coined by Heinrich Woelfflen in his book *Principles of Art History* published in 1915. The word is used to describe the rendering of masses in terms of colour, tone, light and shade, in contrast to 'linear' which concerns statement in terms of contour. Although the word is indicative of the painter's handling of colour and brush, a painterly attitude may sometimes be discerned in line drawing with pencil, pen or etching needle where a close network of lines or a sketchy, impressionistic line (Rembrandt, Topolski) depict mass rather than outline.

Painting   Defined simply in terms of its technical requirements, painting consists of the application of pigment to a surface or support. The pigments are tempered or bound with a suitable vehicle such as oil, gum (water colour) or emulsion (tempera) and made workable with a diluent such as turpentine or water, and they are applied usually with a brush but often with a palette knife. The technical problems involved are intricate, and craftsmanship, an essential part of an artist's training, insists upon their mastery.

Such a definition, however, gives no indication of those other problems which concern the artist in conceiving and executing a painting in order that it may possess aesthetic value, and in the light of the many movements which have flourished in the history of the art, it would be difficult to find a formula which would satisfactorily include all schools of thought. Basically, however, most artists attempt to give an illusion of depth, that is to say, to represent objects, real or imagined, in space by line, tone and colour, and to give solidity by means of light and shade. In order that they may be harmoniously arranged, the painter must apply the principles of composition, which require not only that the objects would seem to be satisfactorily related within the picture, but that their actual shapes should make a pattern on the surface of the canvas. There are painters who deliberately ignore the representation of depth in their canvases, and authorities who assert that such works are not paintings but merely decorations, a criticism that would seem to be contradicted by the work of Gauguin, Matisse and other eminent moderns.

Colour is not always used for imitative purposes, being required by many artists to express a harmonious relationship not necessarily found in nature, some going so far as to produce works of an abstract nature based almost entirely on colour. In fact so subtle are the values of colour against colour that it might be suggested that the whole art of painting, as opposed to drawing, consists entirely in this arrangement of pigments — the re-creation of a natural scene, or the translation of an imaginary idea, in terms of paint.

Painting Knife   See PALETTE KNIFE.

Palace School of Charlemagne   A Carolingian school of miniature painters and illuminators which flourished in the early part of the 9th cent.

Palaeolithic   See PREHISTORIC ART.

Palette   This expression often refers, not merely
to the board on which the artist lays his pigment,
but to the combination of colours which he habitually
uses.   The history of the palette in this sense is
linked very closely with the history of painting as a
whole, as the progressive availability of a greater
range of more brilliant and more permanent pigments
has either assisted the painter in achieving better
effects of naturalism on the one hand, or in
exploiting the purely formal and abstract nature of
colour on the other.   This is not to argue that more
and better pigments are essential for greater works
of art — the painters of ancient Greece e.g. created
masterpieces with a four-colour palette, white, black,
yellow-ochre and a red earth-colour, and Mediaeval
painters were scarcely better off with a larger variety
of low-toned earth-colours and a limited range of
bright colours of animal and vegetable origin and
of very doubtful permanence.   These colours were
divided into two sets, according to brilliance,
austere and *florid*.

Modern chemistry has provided the modern
painter with a choice of approximately 450 different
pigments, and it is from this range that he selects
his palette.   Although a painter can, and frequently
does, arrange a different palette for each projected
picture, the majority are conservative, and having
found by experience those pigments that suit them
best, adhere more or less rigidly to the same set of
colours.   Mr. Hilaire Hiler in his book *Notes on the
Technique of Painting* gives a list of the palettes of
many famous artists.

Palette Knife   This tool is, of course, used
mainly by the artist for mixing his colours on the
palette, but its use has been developed by many
artists as a means of applying the pigment to the
support, and special forms of the tool, known as

painting knives, are manufactured in various shapes and sizes. The characteristic effect of this technique is one of broad tonal values obtained by heavy impasto, but an artist will often execute quite delicate work with considerable detail by using the point of the knife. This method was extensively used by Courbet and many of the Impressionist painters.

Papier Collé   A technique similar to *collage* (q.v.) from which it differs in that the materials are employed primarily for their texture or pattern instead of for their representative and associative values.

Paranoic Criticism   A term used by the Surrealist Salvador Dali to describe the symbolic recording of obsessions, fetishes and hallucinations in his paintings.

Parian Marble   A marble quarried in the island of Paros, from which the finest Greek statues were carved. It is a material ideally suited to the representation of warm vitality, as it contains coarse crystals which reflect the light with a luminous glow.

Partridge Breast   A term applied to a special glaze of light streaks seen on *Temmoku* ware.

Pastel   A softer kind of coloured crayon, bound with just sufficient gum to give shape to the sticks. Drawings in this medium are typically delicate in colour and atmospheric in effect. Some pastels are soluble in water and give an appearance of water colour painting when the drawing is worked over with a wet brush.

Pastiche   In art the selection by an artist of mannerisms in the work of others from which he evolves an individual style but to which he contributes little or nothing original.

Pâte-Sur-Pâte   In ceramics, the application, over a dark ground of successive layers of decoration in white or coloured slips.

Patina   The surface corrosion on antique metal objects caused by the action of the atmosphere or the soils in which they have been buried. Most typical is the bluish green of bronzes, although nearly every hue is to be found according to the metal and the particular conditions to which it has been subjected. The effect is quite often simulated on modern statuary.

Pattern   A harmonious arrangement of the elements in a design or composition.   In its simplest form pattern is the repetition of one or more motifs in a regular scheme as applied to textiles, basket-work etc. But when used in the art of painting, the expression refers to symmetrical or unsymmetrical disposition of lines, shapes and colour to form a balanced composition within the frame of the picture.

Paysage   French for a landscape picture.

Peasant Art   The naive, non-academic, untrained art of unsophisticated communities, producing articles of traditional design and pattern by traditional techniques.   Peasant art is essentially unoriginal, and is the product of the craftsman rather than the artist and expresses local and regional peculiarities rather than national characteristics. Objects of utility are its principle concern, utensils, furniture and dress, and it is rarely concerned with the beautiful for its own sake.

Peinture Claire   An oil paint technique specifically associated with Edouard Manet who painted in the light passages of his pictures first and then, while the pigment was still wet, added the darker tones— a method which was the exact opposite of the current academic practice.

Pen Process Aquatint   A combined etching and aquatint process which allows the reproduction of pen or brush drawings made directly on the plate. The process was used with success by Gainsborough in the 18th century, since when it fell into disuse until revived in recent times by artists anxious to experiment with unusual techniques.

Pentimento　　　　When an artist paints over an original idea it often happens that owing to the tendency for paint to become more transparent with time this first painting frequently shows through. This effect is known as pentimento.

Perception　　　　The artistic faculty for recognising the aesthetic significance of aspects of the visual world which can be conveyed to the spectator by an act of creation.

Period Vision　　　　A phrase used by Mr. Eric Newton to account for the stylistic differences in the representational art of different periods. His theory states that although the mechanical vision of all artists in all ages is the same, there is a censorship in the brain which accepts only a certain amount of visual information as usable material, thus restricting the degree to which the intellectual perception may be visualized. This attitude develops from age to age through innovations by original artists gradually modifying this mental censorship and forming a series of fresh *period visions*. (See Eric Newton's *European Painting and Sculpture*, p. 72, Penguin Books, 1941).

Permanent Colours　　　　Colours which are proof against the action of time and the effects of dampness, light and atmospheric impurities. Furthermore, some otherwise permanent colours are liable to chemical change and discoloration when in contact with certain others, as in the case of vermilions and cadmiums with emerald green for example. The range of permanent colours, which are mainly mineral in origin, has been widened by the discoveries of modern chemistry. The artist who would "paint for posterity" must be fully aware of the potential behaviour of the pigments he would employ and use them accordingly.

Perpendicular Style　　　　The last phase of Gothic architecture which prevailed mainly during the 15th century, in which the vertical tendency of Gothic is emphasised and ornamentation is elaborated.

Perspective   The third dimension may be represented in a drawing or painting by the application of the principles of perspective which are based on the commonly observed phenomena that objects tend to appear smaller as they recede from the eye of the observer, and that receding lines appear to converge upon one or two common vanishing points.

Petite Nature   A French expression for paintings in which figures are so represented as to appear of natural size although their proportions are in fact a little less than life.

Petuntse   Clay obtained from felspar rock, less decayed than *kaolin* (q.v.) and fusible, used as a fusing agent in the manufacture of Chinese porcelain. The name is the French corruption of the Chinese 'Pai-tun-tzu' meaning 'little white blocks', so called because of the pulverized form in which the material was delivered to the potter.

Phelloplastic   A figure or model in cork.

Philistine   Mr. R. H. Wilenski has defined this valuable word as '' . . . . . . the man who is obstinately determined to remain within his familiar experience in every field, holding any further experience to be quite unnecessary; he is the man whose normal impulses towards further experience of any kind have become atrophied; he is the man who has reached a point in his development where he says to himself; 'This is enough. I am what I am. I know what I know. I like what I like. I do not desire to alter in any way'.''

Photographic Tone-Painting   A method of painting in which, by half-closing his eyes, the artist attempts to see the objects before him as a pattern made up of degrees of light as in a photograph. A picture thus conceived usually results in a graduated series of tinted greys, as any attempt to emphasise the local colours might upset the tonal balance.

Photoxylography Process in which the design is photographed on wood for the wood engraver.

Picasso The history and development of the art of Pablo Picasso may be said, almost without exaggeration, to be that of modern art from Post-Impressionism to the present day, and for that reason it may be worth while to list the more important periods of his career.

Born in 1881, Picasso was painting academically and exhibiting in Spain at the age of fourteen. During his frequent visits to Paris, where he settled in 1903, he came under the influence of Gauguin and Toulouse-Lautrec, and the first distinct 'period' begins with the BLUE PERIOD, 1901-04, so called because of the predominance of blue in his pictures (La femme à la chemise). Then followed his ROSE or PINK PERIOD, 1904-5, when the predominant colour of his work changed from blue to pink (L'acrobate à la boule). During these years Picasso's subjects were romantic in theme, beggars, musicians, women and children and later 'saltim-banques' or circus performers.

But the influence of negro sculpture caused him to reject his previous work as sentimental, and (1906-7) the NEGRO PERIOD followed (Danseuse Nègre). Picasso next came under the influence of Cézanne and, together with Braque, he inaugurated the Cubist Movement. His work during this period falls into various categories. The application of Cézanne's ' sphere, cone and cylinder ' dictum produced 'Les bols' in 1907, and the beginnings of abstraction in 1908-9 led to 'La femme au miroir'. 1911 saw the beginning of an almost abstract Cubist period which lasted until the 1920's. About the same time he began to experiment with collage (Journaux et violin, 1912) and in 1917 he began to apply Cubist principles to ballet, designing for Diaghilev and the Russian Ballet.

From 1920 Picasso associated himself with the Surrealist movement, painting in a variety of manners which ranged from the 'antique' style of 'Femmes effrayées au bord de la mer' 1923 and his 'Dinard' paintings of 1928 to the well-known 'Guernica' cf 1937 in which he expressed his disgust with the Spanish Civil War.

Picasso has experimented with Cubist and Surrealist sculpture and has also produced sensitive line drawings of his friends such as 'Stravinsky' 1920 which foreshadowed his CLASSIC PERIOD of 1923 which was inspired by a study of Ingres 'Le repos de l'acrobate'.

The latest phase of his painting is represented by his 'Antibes' pictures, huge works in line and simple colour in which centaurs, disporting themselves in the Mediterranean sea and sun, are the central theme. His most recent work, however, has been in the production of ceramics which, like everything he touches, bear the stamp of his remarkable originality.

Pictography   The art of conveying ideas by means of pictures, signs or symbols suggestive of an object or an idea. This primitive form of writing is the basis of the Egyptian hieroglyphics, and a more undeveloped form is found in the picture writing of the North American Indians.

Picturesque   The representation of nature in a painting in an exaggeratedly sentimental or romantic style.

Pieta   Any religious picture or sculpture representing the Virgin mourning over the dead body of Christ. A motif first found in German art of the 13th century.

Pigment   The colouring matter used by the painter, which usually exists as a powder and is prepared for use by binding with a vehicle such as oil, gum or emulsion.

Pinx. abbreviation of **Pinxit** (Latin meaning "he painted it") The expression is commonly found at the foot of line engravings, signifying the authorship of the original from which the engraving was made. Also found on paintings before the name of the artist.

Pisciform Fish-shaped.

Pittura Metafisica (It. Metaphysical painting) An Italian movement in painting begun by Chirico and Carra in 1915 and which lasted until 1919. This 'Metaphysical' movement was a reaction against the violence and turmoil of *Futurism* (q.v.) and sought instead "the characteristics of the spiritual form" by concentration on still-life subjects. Other Italian painters who came under the influence of the movement were Mario Sironi, Giorgio Morandi and Ardengo Soffici.

Plane of Unsuitability The unusual setting of incongruous objects as depicted in Neo-Surrealist Collage, e.g. "the chance meeting, on a dissecting table, of a sewing machine and an umbrella".

Planes The interrelation of planes (or two-dimensional areas) is one of the fundamental problems of composition. The surfaces of objects may be regarded as so many more or less simple planes which, according to their position (vertical, horizontal or oblique) in relation to the source of illumination, reflect light in varying degrees, thus modifying colour and tone values. Observation of this phenomenon assists the artist in accurately representing three-dimensional space. Cézanne was particularly concerned with the investigation of planes, breaking up his surfaces into smaller facets in order to interpret more accurately the structure behind natural appearances. The results of his researches led the way to Cubist and Abstract experiments in which, when not concerned with representing nature, the artists constructed their planes by means of colour relationships and contrasts. In representational painting and drawing, the depicting of three-dimensional objects upon a two-dimensional surface takes place on the 'picture' plane (which is, of course, no more than the surface of the canvas or other support in use) and the academic artist usually resorts to the use of other imaginary planes, parallel to the picture plane, in order to aid his representation of depth, such planes being usually referred to as Distance and Middle Distance. This device is frequently adapted by semi-abstract painters such as Ben Nicholson, who often reduces his compositions to two-dimensional shapes disposed upon a number of receding planes parallel with the surface of the canvas. Certain Cubist painters, however, rejected the representation of depth in their pictures, in which case their compositions were regarded as being on one plane only, from which the shapes depicted could project but not recede.

Plastic Arts　　　　Those arts concerned with the manipulation of materials into various shapes. The term is usually applied to sculpture and ceramics but also includes the art of oil painting or painting in any medium where the pigment is similarly manipulated.

Plastic Colour　　　　A term coined by Roger Fry to describe colour when it is used to indicate depth and tone in a painting as opposed to its flat decorative use.

Plasticity　　　　This word is used with the greatest looseness by art critics, and its precise meaning frequently has to be determined by the context in which it is used. The general meaning of the word when applied to painting can be sensed from the basic term 'plastic', meaning that which can be modelled or shaped, and it might be said that in order to display 'plasticity' in his work a painter must have the same sense of his medium as the sculptor has for the clay which he manipulates with his hands. Out of the confused application of the term two fairly clear definitions arise, (a) That quality in a painting which reveals the artist's deep feeling for his medium and which results in the use of the inherent qualities of paint, viscosity, pliability and luminosity, to further the aesthetic value of the work, (b) The illusion of solidity, achieved by modelling in paint.

Plein Air (From the French phrase "en plein air" — "in the open air") An expression used to describe the practice of painting in the open in order to catch effects of light and atmosphere unobtainable in the studio. Although the painters of the *Barbizon School* (q.v.) pioneered the practice, the expression is usually associated with the *Impressionists* (q.v).

Pointillism A method of painting invented by Seurat and used by the French Neo-Impressionist painters. The technique was a more logical extension of the Impressionist colour theory, and consisted of the application of the colour of the *spectrum palette* (q.v.) in minute touches to the support in order to effect an optical mixing, which resulted in colours more brilliant and luminous than those obtained by ordinary methods.

Polychromatic Sculpture Sculpture to which colour has been applied in order to give a higher degree of naturalism.

Polynesian Art See OCEANIC PRIMITIVE ART.

Popular Art Art which keeps within the range of commonplace experience, produced either by original artists for mercenary reasons or by unoriginal artists who are incapable of better work.

Porcelain   The finest variety of *stoneware* (q.v.) made originally in China and introduced in quantity into Europe during the 17th century (where it became esteemed as highly as the finest silverware) being successfully imitated during the 18th century at *Sèvres* (q.v.) and Meissen (see DRESDEN CHINA) after a long history of more or less abortive attempts in Europe generally.   True Chinese Porcelain is manufactured from a white refractory (non-fusible) clay known as *Kaolin* fused with a material of similar origin, *Petuntse* (qq.v.), and the unadulterated use of these two ingredients is the reason why this ware is known as 'natural porcelain' (in China, Kaolin and Petuntse are known as "the bones and the flesh" of porcelain).   The earlier European imitations used ground glass as a fusing agent in order to obtain the translucency characteristic of the original product, and they were finished with lead glazes.   Modern English porcelain (known as china) is also of mixed composition, using bone ash with the clay and a lead glaze.

Post-Impressionism   Mr. Roger Fry originated this term to describe an exhibition of paintings which he sponsored in 1910-11 and which, officially titled "Manet and the Post-Impressionists", included, in addition to works by Manet, paintings by Cézanne, Van Gogh, Gauguin, Seurat, Signac, Redon and Denis, sculpture by Maillol and works by Matisse, Rouault and the Fauves.   Picasso and the Cubists were not represented, but were included in the Second Post-Impressionist Exhibition in 1912.

The expression, therefore, describes the movement in modern art which reacted against Impressionist naturalism and concerned itself with the formal aspect of painting as expressed in the work of the painters of the *Modern Classical Renaissance* (q.v.). Although the exhibitions included work by Matisse and Picasso and their associates, certain authorities describe Post-Impressionism as only the work of

Cézanne, Van Gogh and their contemporaries, and maintain that Fauvism and Cubism are the movements by which it was succeeded.

Pottery   Pottery has been described as the most abstract of the arts, and it must be allowed that its freedom from the necessity of representation allied to the most elementary functional requirements permits full expression of purely formal qualities. In the primitive method of manufacture, pottery was built up of coils of clay, and in more recent and commercialised times it has been moulded and cast. But no method can better express the intimate relation between artist and material than the traditional use of the potter's wheel, upon which the work is 'thrown'. After the vessel is formed, it is hardened by 'firing' or baking in a kiln, and the two divisions into which pottery is classified depends upon the degree of heat thus applied. In the case of ordinary *earthenware*, the heat is just sufficient to harden the ware and yet leave it porous. The temperature to which *stoneware* is submitted, however, is sufficient to vitrify the material and render the vessel impervious to liquids, a process which requires the addition of a flux to the material. The porosity of earthenware is overcome by the addition of *glaze* (q.v.) which is only added to stoneware for decorative purposes. Glazes are coloured by means of metallic oxides to which the 'palette' of the potter is limited as other pigments would be discoloured by the great heat of the firing. Pottery is also decorated by *slip, graffito* (qq.v.) and incising.

The form of pottery is either classical, i.e. following Greek principles of flawless symmetry as in most European ware, or vital and organic as in Oriental ware, where irregularity of shape and colour is valued—in some Japanese work to the extent of deliberately marring its symmetry. See PORCELAIN.

Pre-Columbian Art   See AMERICAN ABORIGINAL ART.

Predella   Properly, the step on which an altar is based, but also used to describe the base on which the main panels of an altarpiece are fixed.   Artistically, the term is applied to the pictures or decorations which it was the custom to make on the predella.

Prehistoric Art   Although the period known as Prehistoric covers a vast reach of time, from earliest man until the first civilizations of Egypt, Mesopotamia, Crete and the Indus Valley, we usually associate with 'prehistoric art' the products of the Later Palæolithic, or Old Stone Age.

Sculpture was probably the form of man's earliest attempts at representational art; certainly there are carvings produced by Cro-Magnon Man of the Aurignacian period (approx. 25,000 B.C.) which are far superior in quality to the cryptic and unrealistic cave drawings of the same period. Typical of this type of sculpture is the "Willendorf Venus", a limestone female figure which probably represents the palæolithic ideal of obese feminine beauty. By the time of the Magdalenian period, some 5,000 years later, sculpture had given way to decorative high relief and painting had developed a remarkable realism.

The cave drawings of this period, typified by those in the caverns of Altmira in Spain, may be dismissed by the academic mind as immature artistically and of only scientific interest.   But to the student of modern art they are manifestations of a truly artistic creative ability.   There is no attempt at composition or picture making it is true, as drawing after drawing is executed haphazardly, at times superimposed one upon the other, but it can be justifiably claimed that no product of modern time has surpassed the skill with which the speed and agility of animals have been captured and recorded in these paintings.

They are executed with slightly varied techniques.   The outline is sometimes boldly drawn in black and sometimes firmly engraved, and the colouring ranges from simple monochrome washes to vivid effects in red, yellow, brown and black. Many of the drawings are shaded to produce a beautifully modelled and realistic surface.

At approximately the same time, the Capsian culture was producing paintings of a different style altogether. Both human beings and animals are depicted in a fashion which, while not approaching the beauty of the Magdalenian pictures, are convincingly animated.

By the time of the Azilian culture (about 5,000 B.C.) the creative impulse had unfortunately degenerated and survived only in the form of symbolic painting upon pebbles etc. This heralds the approach of the *Neolithic Period* or New Stone Age when Man in his progress towards more settled conditions would seem preoccupied with more material strivings and less concerned with artistic achievements.

Pre-Raphaelite Brotherhood   Name adopted by three British artists, D. G. Rossetti, J. E. Millais and W. Holman Hunt, who in 1848 revolted against contemporary academic art and advocated a return to the simple naturalism of Italian Primitive painters such as Botticelli, Fra Angelico and Fillipo Lippi. They eschewed the use of heavy shadow and painted on a white instead of the usual bitumenous ground of the time, and this, together with the use of bright colours, gave their work a novel brilliance which was greeted by a storm of abuse from a public conditioned to the "old violin" hues of the popular romantic painters.   Although they held these principles in common, the three artists expressed themselves in fundamentally different ways. Millais and Hunt were concerned with aspects of dramatised realism, while Rossetti attempted to give expression to a highly romantic mediaevalism.   The Brotherhood was later joined by several lesser artists including C. G.

Stephens, T. Woolner, W. H. Deverell and J. Collinson, and came to an end in 1853.

Priming   The preliminary oil, glue or gesso ground, applied to a canvas or support to render it suitable for painting on.

Primitive Art   By primitive art is meant the art of prehistoric man and modern savage societies. Such art although primitive in point of time (for recent savage art may be said to be prehistoric in spirit) is from an aesthetic point of view commonly as high and often higher than the art of later civilizations.   Although the primitive artist lacks scientific knowledge (perspective, light and shade etc.) he possesses the ability to transcribe his visual experience directly and almost instinctively.   A complete lack of self-consciousness, in fact, might be said to be the essential quality of primitive art.   The style ranges from the symbolic to a free and vital naturalism.

Child Art (q.v.) is also included under this heading as the child of modern civilization, in the early stages of his mental development, would seem psychologically to have much the same outlook as primitive man.

Peasant Art (q.v.) although possessing much in common with the art of primitive peoples has been largely modified by sophisticated urban art, and has been more accurately described as "derivative art". (See AMERICAN ABORIGINAL ART ; AUSTRALIAN ABORIGINAL ART; BUSHMAN ART; NEGRO ART; OCEANIC PRIMITIVE ART).

The term "primitive" has also been used to describe the early Italian and Flemish painters who, although by no means primitive in the first sense of the word, displayed a certain degree of naivety; and it has also been applied to certain modern painters who evince similar characteristics, e.g. The Douanier Rousseau and Alfred Wallis.

Primitivism   Primitivism is used to describe the
the attitude adopted by many painters of the present
century who, inspired by savage, peasant or child
art, sought to incorporate in their works similar
qualities of unsophisticated vision.   Perhaps the most
successful of these was Paul Gauguin and later
Picasso who were both, however, mainly concerned
with the adaptation of primitive elements for the
purpose of a new formal language in painting.   On
the other hand, certain of their followers attempted
a complete emulation, the futility of which is best
summed up by the words of Ozenfant. "Simplicity,
the moment it becomes an attitude, ceases to exist".
Works of this nature should not be confused with
that of such true modern primitives as Rousseau and
Alfred Wallis.

Problem Picture   A picture whose purpose or
theme is difficult or impossible to decipher.   A
traditional feature of entertainment at the Annual
Exhibition of the Royal Academy.

Psalter   A book of psalms which, like the missal
and similar manuscript books of devotion, has
provided opportunity for much fine work in the art
of illuminating.

Purbeck Marble   A brown limestone obtained from
Purbeck on the Dorset coast.

Pure Colour   See COLOUR.

Purism   In 1918 the French artist Amédée
Ozenfant, who had for some time criticised Cubism
as being largely romantic and decorative in spirit,
developed his own particular variety of *Flat Pattern
Cubism* (q.v.) which he called Purism. His paintings
of 1918-25 are practical examples of his theory
which is explained in the book which he wrote
together with Le Corbusier called *Après la Cubisme*,
1918.   It was the intention of Purism to instil
a more classical or architectural quality into
Cubism, and for this reason his pictures were

constructed by means of "constant universal forms" (See CONSTANTS) and avoided as far as possible purely incidental forms which, Ozenfant maintained, are of purely personal emotional significance (as in much of Picasso's Cubist work). The austere quality of Purism might in the hands of a less accomplished artist have produced pictures of an arid and mechanical nature which the work of Ozenfant avoided by his vital use of line and colour.

Putti (It.) Figures of nude, cupid-like children often found in painting and sculpture of the Italian Renaissance.

Q

Qualities In using this term the critic usually refers to the intrinsic nature of the surface of a picture, the textures of the pigments and their relationship with the canvas or support.

Quattrocento It. for "four hundred", but used for the 15th cent. (i.e. the fourteen hundreds) to describe Italian art of that cent., particularly that of Florence.

R

Rainbow Palette See SPECTRUM PALETTE.

Rajput Painting Rajput painting, which describes the various schools which flourished in Rajputana and the Punjab from the 16th to the 19th cents., is one of the most important aspects of Indian art. While Moghul painting with which it is usually compared, is realistic in outlook, Rajput painting is truly mediaeval in spirit, concerning itself with the illustration of Hindu epic legends in a graceful, linear style, sensitively and translucently coloured.

Rapin French for a painter's pupil. Sometimes used contemptuously to describe a dabbler in painting.

Rayonism   A theory expounded by the Russian Larionov based upon the Impressionist conception of light and modified by Cubist and Futurist principles. Although his theory had no substantial following, Larionov himself had considerable influence on theatre decoration.

Ready Mades   A term used in *Dadaism* (q.v.) to describe a machine-made object selected by the artist and considered by him a work of art by virtue of the fact that it is his perception which has endowed it with aesthetic significance — the act of selection in this case being regarded as a form of creative activity.   Literary titles were sometimes added in which case the Dadaist considered he had created another form, and when further details were added the object was known as *ready-made-aided.*

Realism   Realism in art, in its formal aspect, is concerned with interpreting the essential nature of the subject represented and revealing truths hidden by the *accidentals* (q.v.) of ordinary visual appearances.   To this end, therefore, verisimilitude becomes of secondary importance, as in the work of Cézanne and Van Gogh, for example.   The realistic approach, while observed in much representational art such as that of the 16th cent. in Italy, is also the basis of early Cubist and Abstract painting.   In this sense, Realism is opposed to *Naturalism* (q.v.), but confusion may arise from the use of the expression in another, almost literary, sense, in opposition to Idealism and Romanticism where it is the content rather than the form which is being defined. Realistic art of this nature refers to painting and sculpture where the subject, usually human, is observed objectively and depicted undramatically and often in an almost sordid manner.   See, for example, the work of Brueghel and Flemish painting in general, and also the French Realists of the early 19th cent. Millet, Courbet etc.

It should be noted in addition, that Realism is often used as a synonym for the whole body of Representational Art (q.v.).

Recession   The representation of depth and the illusion of a third dimension in a painting is known as recession, an effect which is usually obtained by the application of the principles of linear and aerial perspective.   In works of an abstract nature, recession may also be produced by the relative behaviour of colours, e.g. the "going back" of a cold grey or blue and the "coming forward" of a warm yellow or red.

Red-Figured Vases   A type of terra-cotta pottery developed by the Athenians towards the close of the 6th cent. B.C. in which the drawing was first incised on the vase and the background filled in with a black glaze, with the result that the figures themselves appeared as red on a black background. This method was far superior to the earlier *black-figured style* (q.v.) in that a greater freedom of drawing was permitted.

Re-Entoilage   In the restoration of oil paintings, the delicate operation of re-canvassing, or removing the actual pigment and re-laying it on a fresh canvas.

Reflected Colour   The modification of the local colour of an object brought about by its reflection of the colour of any object, ground or background in proximity to it.

Reims, School of   A Carolingian school of illuminators and miniature painters where the Ebo Evangeliar and the Utrecht Psalter were written.

Reisner Work   Inlay work using different coloured woods.   A method named after a German wood-worker of the time of Louis XIV.

Relief   A type of sculpture in which the carving projects from and is part of the main body of the stone or wood.   Its main use is in architectural decoration, although the style is also used in such crafts as silver work and the carving of cameos. Relief carving is classified as high or low relief according to the degree to which the work projects from the surface. Where the object depicted projects by no more than half its relative thickness, the work is said to be in *low relief*, where it projects by more than one half it is considered to be in *high relief*. High relief is obtained by extensive "undercutting", but should not be confused with pseudo-relief where the figures are carved in the round and artificially attached to the surface to be decorated.

The term relief is also used to describe the rendering of solidity in painting and drawing.

Religious Art   It is generally held that the Paleolithic cave drawings were prompted by some mystical or religious considerations and the sculpture of most savage communities has a similar origin. Since the earliest times until the Late Renaissance, religion has been, with few exceptions, the greatest outlet for the artist's creativity. When Venice became the centre of the Renaissance, art transferred its allegiance from the Church to the aristocracy and the merchant princes and became a secular activity, and with the waning of the influence of the Church there has been no great religious activity requiring artistic expression. There have been, however, artists with a religious attitude, e.g. Stanley Spencer in England and Georges Rouault in France. In connection with the former, throughout all of whose work there runs a thread of Biblical mysticism, mention should be made of the Burghclere Memorial chapel in Hampshire which was built expressly for Spencer to decorate. Significant also is the gesture of the Vicar of St. Matthew's, Northampton, who commissioned a crucifixion by Graham Sutherland and a Madonna and Child by Henry Moore. Perhaps the most interesting example of contemporary religious art is that of Notre Dame de Toute Grâce at A'ssy Sanatorium in Haute-Savoie. Designed by the architect Maurice Novarina, the church is being decorated by a host of modern French artists — a mosaic facade by Léger, stained glass by Rouault, tapestry by Lurçat, a Virgin & Child by Lipchitz, bronze doors to the tabernacle by Braque and a canvas by Bonnard.

Renaissance Art While the scholar and historian differ in opinion regarding the nature of the spirit which was awakened during the Renaissance, its social implications and even the precise date at which it may be said to emerge from the Gothic period which preceded it, the student of the arts will be concerned principally with the fact that the Renaissance saw the beginning of that tradition in art against which the revolutionary spirit of the 19th and 20th cents. have seen fit to react.

Inspired by the re-discovery of humanistic Classical art, all the artistic genius of the 15th and 16th cents. was bent on expressing itself in terms of more and more accurate representation of human and natural forms. The science of perspective was formulated and applied, human anatomy was investigated, not only for the benefit of science, but towards its more realistic portrayal in art, and chiaroscuro and the study of light and shade eventually led to the production of the completely naturalistic painting, which by the end of the 16th cent. had become the commonly accepted medium for artistic expression.

This intellectual attitude was more characteristic of the *Florentine School* (q.v.) than any other, the earlier *School of Siena* (q.v.) being more Gothic than Renaissance in spirit, and the *Venetian School* (q.v.) was more or less content to utilize the results of Florentine enquiry to express an exuberance of feeling in the recording of the glory of their prosperous city.

Late Renaissance. This period, roughly the late 16th cent., saw the emergence of a variety of styles based on those of the great masters of the High Renaissance, and is remarkable for the appearance of a number of conflicting schools and academies, e.g. *Chiaroscurists, Eclectics, Macchinisti* and *Naturalisti* (qq.v.).

Repoussé   A method of working relief designs in ductile metals such as silver by hammering the reverse side.

Representational Art is that branch of artistic activity in which the artist is concerned with recording his ideas about the visible world, and is therefore roughly the opposite to abstract art although the dividing line between the two is difficult to define, as *Semi-Abstract* and even *Near-Abstract* painting (See ABSTRACT ART) are representational to some degree. It has been held by some authorities that even purely abstract art is representational of the artist's imagination. It is usual, however, to consider representational art as dealing only with the artist's re-creation, or re-presentation, of natural appearances, and in this respect falls mainly into the two divisions of *Naturalism* and *Realism* (qq.v.).

Reredos   An ornamented wall or screen which usually stands out from the wall behind a church altar, although sometimes joined to the wall. The reredos is usually elaborately ornamented with sculpture and tracery and is a particular feature of Spanish church architecture, although there exist some famous examples in English churches and cathedrals, in particular the late 15th cent. specimen at St. Albans.

Retable   A frame enclosing decorated panels above the back of an altar.

Rhenish School   A style of art which developed in the Cologne region during the 12th and early

13th cents. which combined the influences of French, Gothic, German Romanesque and Carolingian Renaissance. The style expressed itself mainly in sculpture, usually in relief, and the best example is the Shrine of the Three Kings in Cologne Cathedral executed by Nicolaus of Verdun *circa* 1200.

Rhyparography   A type of genre painting which depicts mean or sordid subjects.

Rhythm   The word is derived from the Greek "rhein" meaning "to flow" and refers to the unification of a work of art by the repetition of similar elements of line, form and colour. Rhythm of line, of primary importance in draughtsmanship, depends upon an alternate stressing and relaxation expressed by thinness and thickness of stroke, depth and shallowness of curves and the varying breadth of the areas contained in the contours.

Rococco (Fr. *Rocaille*, shell-shaped, a favourite motif in late Baroque ornamentation)   This term first came into use about 1830 to describe the latest phase of Baroque, i.e. from about 1720-1770. About the beginning of the 18th cent. the heavy forms of Baroque began to show an even greater freedom from classical restraint and from utilitarian purpose. The playful vitality of the period began to display itself in a wealth of ornamental inventions, and for the last time an art style was introduced in which sculpture, painting and the decorative arts all expressed the same spirit. In architecture, the true spirit of Rococco is only to be found on the Continent in such cities as Vienna, Munich, Prague and Dresden. In this country the nearest thing to the style is found in the Neo-Classical Palladianism. In painting, the best expression of Rococco is found in the work of the French painters Watteau, Boucher and Fragonard.

Romanesque   The style of architecture prevailing in Europe from the 4th cent. to the 13th, based on the Roman round arch and barrel-vault. In this country the style is known as Norman.

Romanists   The name of a group of Flemish painters who worked in Rome in the 16th and 17th cents. and who were strongly influenced by Raphael and Michelangelo.   They include Van Orley and Franz Floris.

Romantic Art   That form of art which is concerned with the artist's emotions and feelings about his subject rather than with his apprehension of its structural nature, and with the representation of poetic and dramatic qualities rather than with the organisation of a formal unity.   Romantic art in this sense is the opposite of *Classic Art* (q.v.).   But the expression sometimes refers to the theme or subject of a work of art when it is of an emotional or sentimental nature — a theme which may nevertheless be presented in classic form.   This apparent contradiction may be exemplified by reference to French painting of the late 18th cent. and early 19th cent. where the *Neo-Classical School* (q.v.) which was classic in treatment (David, Ingres) was succeeded by the Romantic school which was Romantic in treatment (Delacroix, Gericault), although both schools concerned themselves with romantic themes.

The difference between the romantic and classic artist is largely one of temperament, and the romantic artist is primarily concerned with the expression of his own personality.   The romantic spirit is found most strongly in the northern races which are susceptible to the atmospheric and mystic qualities of nature in their climate.   The history of English art has been almost entirely romantic in outlook and has been largely expressed in landscape painting.   Although in recent years continental influences of a classical nature have been experimented with in this country, the romantic tradition has firmly reasserted itself in the modern English *Neo-Romantic School* (q.v.).

Rood Screen   A richly carved and decorated screen used in the mediaeval church to separate that part of the church reserved for the use of the clergy from that used by the laity.

Rose-Croix Movement   The Rose-Croix Movement was an "Anti-Realist" movement in all the arts (particularly music and the theatre) launched by the French writer "Sar" Péladin in 1892 and which lasted for the remainder of the century. The movement was closely linked with the *Symbolist* and *Nabis* movements (qq.v.) but the emphasis was on the portrayal of "mystical" subjects, and much of the art was devoted to the decoration of theatrical productions. No really important artists were members of the movement, the first and second Rose-Croix Salons of 1897 including works by such painters as Obert and Aman Jean and the engraver, Marcellin Desboutins. In fact, so far as painting is concerned, the movement was a minor one during a period of great artistic activity, and is perhaps not so much notable for the intrinsic value of the work produced as for the fact that, together with that of such "fantastic" painters as Odilon Redon and James Ensor, it was a forerunner of the coming *Surrealist Movement* (q.v.).

Rose Period   See PICASSO.

Rotoreliefs   Series of discs constructed by Marcel Duchamp in 1935 which, placed upon the turntable of a gramophone and revolved, give the optical illusion of movement in three dimensions.

Royal Academy of Arts, The   Founded in London in 1768 under the patronage of George III for the establishment of a school of art and for the annual exhibition of works of contemporary artists. It was first housed in Somerset House until 1869, when the present home at Burlington House was acquired. The Academy holds an annual summer exhibition of pictures, statuary and architectural designs to which anyone can submit.

Rubens School　　　　A 17th cent. school of painting founded by Peter Paul Rubens at Antwerp, which included Van Dyck, Seghers and Snyders.

Russian Futurists, The　　　　A general name for the extreme groups of the Russian adherents to Cubism, Expressionism, etc.

S

St. Gallen, School of　　　　A Carolingian school of illuminators and miniature painters in the early part of the 9th cent.

Salian Art　　　　German art of the period 1024-1137, the epoch of the German Emperors of the Salian Frankish House. The stiff, angular style of paintings of this period found in numerous illuminated manuscripts, was Byzantine in spirit and was a continuation with very little change of the preceding Ottonian period. The most notable event of the period was the use of the vault for the first time in the building of Speyer Cathedral.

Sanguine　　　　A crayon made with red ochre, and one of the earliest of drawing materials. It is used with beautiful effect either alone or in conjunction with *Conté* (q.v.).

Scraperboard　　　　A method of drawing for reproduction utilizing a board coated with a chalk surface which the artist covers with a black wash which is scraped away with an instrument to reveal white lines and areas. The process is similar in effect to a wood engraving, with the difference that it is possible for black lines to be drawn in afterwards.

Sculps.　　　　Abbreviation for Sculpsit (Latin "he carved"). Indicates, on an engraving, the name of the engraver. Also used on sculpture in association with the name of the sculptor.

Sculpture   The art of sculpture is concerned with carving or modelling in wood, stone, ivory, clay, and metal, in the round or in relief. It has, with painting, been a means of self-expression to mankind since the earliest times, either for magical and religious purposes or for purely aesthetic creation.

Most sculpture until recent times has been representational in kind, but, as in the graphic arts, the attitude of the sculptor has varied from the highly naturalistic to the symbolic, a range of ideas which still provides scope for talented work to-day. The last half-century, however, has seen the experiments of modern art echoed in the sphere of sculpture, particularly in the field of abstract composition, the extreme expression of which is probably to be found in the work of the *Constructivists* (q.v.) with their *equipoised* and *kinetic* sculpture (qq.v.). Although modelling and carving which is purely imitative in interest is produced (wax works and showroom models) they have little aesthetic value and can hardly merit the title of sculpture. Sculpture, in fact, has a deeper purpose than the merely imitative, and although authorities contend among themselves regarding the precise nature of this purpose, we may accept that sculpture in the round should be aesthetically pleasing when looked at from any angle and, except in the case of relief, should not be conceived from one particular aspect. Certain archaic sculpture was executed as seen from the front, and even when this attitude was overcome the sculptor conceived his statue from four points only, front, sides and back. Not until the classical age did the Greeks realise the ideal statue, having a complete three-dimensional existence.

Modern sculptors assert that their work should be conceived as an organic whole, not as a synthesis of an infinite number of aspects, and enthusiasts for negro and Polynesian sculpture claim that it is this attitude which the savage craftsman possesses (consciously or unconsciously) to a high degree.

Sculpture requires also that the artist should be aware of the potentialities of his material—that stone carving should not be used to render the slender limbs and draperies for which bronze is so satisfactorily suited. Henry Moore, for example, sets out to translate the human organism into stone as he thinks nature would work upon the material, and in so doing he applies the knowledge gained from the observation and study of pebbles, rocks, caves and hills. Brancusi, Lipchitz, Archipenko, Arp, Hepworth, Zadkine are abstract sculptors, and the leaders of the *Constructivists* are Gabo and Pevsner. Giacometti is a Surrealist sculptor, while Maillol, Despiau, Epstein, and Mestrovic are acknowledged leaders in a more academic field.

Sculpturesque Painters See DIRECT PAINTING, SCHOOL OF.

Scumbling The application of light, opaque pigment over a darker colour in order to lighten it. Pigment applied in this fashion is of a dry consistency and it is rubbed on in order to allow patches of the colour beneath to show through. The result is a rough texture which often possesses a pleasant quality in itself. Scumbling is the reverse procedure to *glazing* (q.v.).

Secret Decoration A very fine form of engraving on certain examples of Chinese porcelain, so called because the decoration is only perceptible in a very strong light.

Seicento (It. short for *mil seicento*, one thousand six hundred). The 17th cent. period of Italian art.

Semi-Abstract See ABSTRACT ART.

Sepia Drawing A method of line and wash drawing executed in brown monochrome. The name derives from the original use of sepia, a pigment obtained from the ink bag of the cuttle fish.

Serigraphy   The name given to the silk screen process when used as a fine art reproduction medium.

Seven and Five Society   This group was founded by a number of young artists shortly after the first world war, and took its name from the fact that it was composed of seven painters and five sculptors, which included H. S. Williamson, P. H. Jowett, Claude Flight and Ivon Hitchens. In those early days the members would seem to have had no common idea other than the wish to exhibit, nor was their work particularly advanced. The year 1925, however, saw the introduction of Ben and Winifred Nicholson into the group, and with the continued intake of more advanced members (and the corresponding resignations of others), the style became progressively abstract.

The Exhibitions, which were now held at the Liecester Galleries, were representative of the most stimulating and advanced work in the country, by a list of artists which included such names as John Piper, Ivon Hitchens, David Jones, Cedric Morris, Staite Murray (potter), John Skeaping, Christopher Wood, Henry Moore, Barbara Hepworth, and the Nicholsons.

The Society does not appear to have been officially dissolved, but with the success of its leading members and the outbreak of war, exhibiting has unfortunately been discontinued, and no other group which can adequately replace it has come into existence.

Sèvres Ware   Porcelain produced at Sèvres in France, particularly the soft-paste porcelain (an attempt to imitate true Chinese porcelain) under the Royal directorship of Louis XV during the late 18th cent. It was more fragile than the Chinese ware and extremely costly to produce. The style might best be described as Rococco, being elaborately decorated and painted with highly naturalistic pictures. The best examples were produced prior to about 1756 after which date the Louis Seize style was introduced under the influence of the Neo-Classical revival, which resulted in attempts to imitate bronze, gilt, marble, etc. to the detriment of its natural porcelain form.

Sezession 1894   A German Impressionist movement which revolted in 1894 against the academic tradition of the "Glaspalast". Liebermann, Slevogt and Corinth are the artists most prominently associated with the movement.

Sfregazzi (It.)   A method of glazing shadows over flesh tints, effected by drawing the finger, dipped in the darker colour, over the area to be shaded.

Sfumato (It. smoked)   The softening and blending of light tones into dark, often productive of a 'vapoury' quality. Probably the most notable use of this method is found in the painting of Leonardo.

Sgraffito   See GRAFFITO.

Siena, School of   An early school of Italian painting which expressed the earlier spirit of the Italian Renaissance in art. The art of this city flourished in the late 13th and 14th cents., after which it was overshadowed by the greatness of Florence. Sienese painting, inspired by an almost mediaeval devoutness, possessed a sweetness of expression and a decorative feeling in composition, unlike the vigorous, realistic outlook of its more forward-looking neighbour Florence. Duccio di Buoninsegna (1278-1319) was the first Sienese painter of note, and the school took definite shape under the leadership of Simone Martini (1283-1344).

Significant Form   A term coined by Mr. Clive Bell and first used by him in his book *Art* published in 1914, to describe the fundamental quality common to all works of visual art, the quality that is shared by all objects that provoke aesthetic emotion. This theory implies that Chartres Cathedral, a T'ang horse, a Constable landscape, a Picasso and a piece of sculpture by Henry Moore, all have some basic quality in common as works of art.

Silver Point　　　　A method of drawing using an instrument tipped with silver upon a slightly abrasive surface or a paper impregnated with zinc white. Silver point drawing requires great discipline as it is impossible to erase, but produces a more delicate effect than the finest lead pencil drawing.

Simultanéisme　　　　In 1913, the Cubist painter Robert Delaunay, inspired by Italian *Futurism* (q.v.), painted a series of pictures embodying fragments of revolving discs with which he attempted to convey a sense of movement. These experiments he called *Simultanéisme* and they were also notable for the fact that Delaunay and his group reverted from the prevailing phase of monochrome painting in Cubism to the use of bright colour, for which reason the writer Apollinaire re-christened the movement *Orphism* meaning thereby an art of pure and abstract colour.

Simultaneity　　　　The expression 'simultaneity' is used in both the theories of *Cubism* and *Futurism* but with quite different meanings. In *Cubism* it describes the representation of different aspects of an object in a single composition in order to convey a fuller statement about the object portrayed. In *Futurism*, on the other hand, simultaneity endeavours to portray movement by depicting a sequence of positions, e.g. Balla portrays in one of his pictures a multiple-legged figure in order to suggest the action of walking.

Sketch　　　　A rapid drawing or painting lacking in detail and intending to convey a general impression of an object or scene, or of an intended project. Sketches are often esteemed as works of art in themselves, and in the case of certain artists, such as Constable and Turner, are sometimes held to be of greater aesthetic value than the artist's finished works.

Slip   Liquid clay used for decorative purposes in pottery, either applied as a complete covering by dipping (when it may sometimes be cut or scratched away to reveal underlying material) or applied by brush in a decorative design.

Soviet Realism   The degenerate, state-sponsored "art" of Soviet Russia, mainly concerned with portraits of national heroes and executed in a meretricious, naturalistic style.

Space   Broadly, space is the whole surface of the picture upon which masses are disposed, or the volume in which they exist when the picture aims at representing depth. Space is negative mass, and in the composition of a picture may be regarded as having the same function as rests in music.

Spanish Art   Although there is no country whose art has a stronger national flavour than that of Spain, there was no truly national school of painting in that country before the 17th cent. Spanish painting of that cent. centres round the two great names of El Greco (1548? - 1614 or 25) and Velasquez (1599-1660), and the three lesser artists Zurbaran (1598-1664), Ribera (1588 - 1652) and Murillo (1617-1682). From thence until the advent of Goya (1746 - 1828) there was nothing distinctly national or outstanding in merit in Spanish art, and after Goya there was again almost complete obscurity until Picasso.

In spite of the brevity and intermittency of these flowerings, the work associated with these few names is of the greatest importance in the history of European art. El Greco, an Italian-trained Greek domiciled in Spain, was one of the most powerfully individualistic artists of all time. By a unique style, in which extreme distortion of the human form was an important element, El Greco convincingly expressed the ecstacies of Spanish Christian mysticism. The work of Velasquez, on the other hand, is characterised by a calm, detached objectivity of vision rendered with exquisite painterly skill. Ribera developed a high degree of realistic skill and used it to portray brutal and gruesome themes which, unreasonable as it seems, somehow detracts from the value of his genius. Zurbaran also pursued a naturalistic technique but, in contrast to Ribera, used it to impart realism to scenes of mystical experience. Murillo, an artist with less distinction than any of the others, modelled his style on the work of Titian and Van Dyck, and produced an immense amount of work largely for church decoration.

Francisco Goya, a truly Spanish temperament of violent passions and macabre fantasies, arose out of the dull mediocrity of foreign inspired 18th cent. Spanish painting, and developed a fully individual style whose sources he claimed to find in Velasquez, Rembrandt and Nature. Although Goya is principally noted for his portrayal of the grim and savage aspects of human behaviour, he was also a portrait painter of exceptional ability with a shrewd and satirical eye that sometimes brought his likenesses near to satire.

In the world of modern art, Spain has no outstanding indigenous school, but Picasso, a Spaniard by birth, has made a larger contribution to art than any other living painter, and two more Spaniards, Juan Gris and Joan Miro, have played important parts in the development of the Modern Movement.

Spectrum Palette also known as **Rainbow Palette**
The use of pigments corresponding as closely as possible to the colours found in the spectrum of sunlight. It was first used in a limited way by the French painter Renoir and by the Impressionist painters generally. It was later used by Seurat and

his followers in a scientific manner, i.e. he used only the spectrum colours and applied them purely in minute touches. See POINTILLISM.

Sphere, Cone and Cylinder   In April, 1904, the French painter Paul Cézanne said in a letter to a friend "all nature models itself on the *sphere, the cone and the cylinder*. Learn to paint these simple shapes and you will afterwards be able to do whatever you wish". The *Post-Impressionists* (q.v.) seized upon this dictum as the basis for their approach, and Picasso in 1907 founded upon it his earliest experiments in *Cubism* (q.v.).

Stabiles   A name given by the American artist, Alexander Calder, to his "Static Abstract Sculptures" as distinct from his Mobiles or "plastic forms in motion". See KINETIC SCULPTURE.

Stämning (Swedish)   The spiritual mood of landscape, a characteristic of Scandinavian painting.

Steel Engraving   See LINE ENGRAVING.

Sterochromy, Mineral Painting or Water-Glass Painting A comparatively new method of painting, particularly suitable for mural decoration, which uses water-glass as a medium. The value of this method is due to the insolubility of water-glass after hardening. The pigments which are the same as those used in fresco are mixed with water-glass and applied to the dry plaster, after which the whole painting is thoroughly drenched with the water-glass solution.

Stiacciato (It.)   Exceptionally low relief.

Still Life or **Nature Morte**   The use of inanimate objects as subjects for pictures, extensively used by painters of the modern schools since inanimate subjects lend themselves more readily to purely formal compositions.

Stipple   (1) In painting a method of obtaining a uniform slightly textured or "dotted" surface by a regular "dabbing" with the point of the brush.

The method is also used to work two or more colours together to obtain a desired effect, as, for example, foliage.

(2) In pen and ink drawing a method of representing gradations of tone by the use of dots in a closely-woven texture. Also, a similar process employed in certain kinds of engraving (etching, wood engraving etc.).

Stoneware One of the two main divisions of pottery, the other being *Earthenware* (q.v.). The clay used for stoneware contains a flux so that in firing the material fuses, resulting in a vessel vitreous and non-absorbent. Glaze is added for decorative purposes only.

Strapwork A method of ornamentation found on illuminated manuscripts of the 15th and 16th cents., consisting of intricately interwoven bands.

Studio Potter An artist engaged in the production of highly individual pottery in contrast to the commercial productions of the factories, e.g. Bernard Leach at St. Ives, Cornwall.

Study A drawing or painting made with care (either imaginatively or from nature) for purposes of study or as a preparation for a projected work of art.

Stump An instrument of rolled chamois leather or parchment, pointed at one end, which is used for blending and softening the tones in pastel, crayon and charcoal drawings.

Style Flamboyant The third period of French Gothic architecture, equivalent to the English Perpendicular Style, from which it differs, however, in several important aspects. The name derives from the flame-like nature of the tracery.

Style Mécanique, Le A popular name given in the 1920's to a style in architecture, interior decoration, dress design etc., which was inspired by the severe principles of *Functionalism* and *Purism* (qq.v.).

In its most debased form it was known as *Le Style Jazz*.

Style Rayonnant   The second period of French Gothic architecture, equivalent to the English Decorated.

Subject   The subject of a work of art may be on the one hand its actual *raison d'être*, or on the other merely an excuse for the artist to bring together his ideas of composition or to record his observation. In the most abstract work, the structural problems which the artist has solved and the visual truths which he has presented, may be regarded as the subject matter, but the more obvious use of the word usually refers to that which the picture is 'about'. In this sense the subject of the picture is probably of more importance to the spectator than to the artist himself. Nevertheless, until the most recent years the painter and sculptor have always seen fit to record some aspect of nature, and for the greater part of the history of art, man has been the subject of greatest importance. Landscapes, however, originally the background for the display of human figures, eventually achieved emancipation during the 18th and 19th cents. and together with still-life developed into subject matter in its own right. Except in the case of such abstract painters as Hélion and Mondriaan, the most advanced Cubist, Expressionist and Fauvist painting has always adhered to the subject even when distorted or disintegrated, and now that the most violent experiments of the century would appear to have been carried out and their results assimilated, the subject is regaining its position of importance in the work of the most significant painters of the day, e.g. Colquhoun, McBryde, Minton, etc.

Sunday Painters   This was originally a French expression for the amateur who devoted his spare time to painting. The cult is widespread throughout the world, however, and the term has recently come into vogue in the U.S.A. where amateur painting is a highly popular form of hobby. Most Sunday Painters are, of course, unschooled and technically unaccomplished, but this is by no means the rule. Mr. Winston Churchill, for example, is not only a distinguished Sunday Painter, but has also written *Painting as a Pastime* to recommend its pursuit. See UNSCHOOLED PAINTERS.

Sung Art   The art of China during the Sung Dynasty (960-1280 A.D.), a period of great philosophic and literary as well as artistic activity. Sung landscape painting is the product of this philosophic and poetic attitude and expressed itself with charm of surface and technique but lacked the power and feeling of earlier dynastic painting. Similarly in sculpture, simple formalism gave way to increasing naturalism and graceful elaboration. It is in the realm of ceramics, however, that the Sung Dynasty excels. Sung pottery shows a preoccupation with form, decoration being limited to simple monochrome glazes and occasional restrained incised design. The most outstanding work of this dynasty is perhaps the Celadon porcelains in which the potter would seem to have attempted the imitation of jade.

Super-Realism   An alternative but little used term for *Surrealism* (q.v.) which is an anglicised form of the French *Surréalisme*. The French prefix 'sur' is however, more accurately translated into English by 'super'.

Support   A general term for any material, canvas, wood, metal, paper, board etc. upon which a work of art is produced.

Suprematism   A movement originated by the Russian Kasamir Malevich in 1913 which he exemplified by the exhibition of a picture of a black square on a white ground to demonstrate his "system of absolutely pure geometric abstraction".

Malevich explained his theory in a book titled
"The Non-Objective World" which was published
by the Bauhaus in 1927.

Among Malevich's followers were Rodchenko,
Puni, Rosanova, Lissitzky, Exter and Drevin.
Suprematism and *Tatlinism* (q.v.), a parallel movement which totally rejected the traditional canvas,
both developed in due course into *Constructivism*
(q.v.).

Surface   The organisation of the surface of
his canvas is not the least of the problems that beset
the artist.   In normal representational art, the
painter must compose shapes that not only serve
to represent objects in three-dimensional space, but
which fit together to provide a harmonious pattern
of the two-dimensional surface which is bounded
by the frame.   This task is so difficult that many
painters are liable to emphasise one of these aspects
of composition at the expense of the other.   Only in
the work of a master is there found this ability to
compose equally in depth and on the surface.

The surface finish of a picture results from the
handling of the pigment and varies with the different
types of brushwork used (the smooth finish of
Vermeer and the broad impasto of Van Gogh), with
the use of scumble or glaze, and with the use of
tools other than the brush — the vigorous technique
of the palette knife and the infinite number of
textures obtained by scratching and rubbing on the
canvas or wood of the support.

Surrealism   The aim of Surrealism is to overcome
the barriers which exist between the conscious and
the unconscious mind and between the 'real' and
'unreal' worlds of waking and dreaming.   The term
Surnaturel, subsequently altered to Surrealism, was
first applied in 1912 by Guillaume Apollinaire to
certain works by the painter Marc Chagall who
used subject matter of a dreamlike nature, e.g.

animals with transparent abdomina and humans with heads reversed upon their shoulders. Giorgio di Chirico was at the same time independently pursuing similar aims by producing works which suggested states of 'disquietude' or not unpleasant feelings of uneasiness, as for example a statue in a deserted street with a long arcaded perspective. This cult of what has been described as "irrational fantasy" was not, however, without precedent, being to some extent heralded by the work, during the last quarter of the 19th cent. of Gustave Moreau, Odilon Redon, James Ensor and the *Rose-Croix* "mystic" painters, the literary inspiration of Huysmans and Péladin, and later by the work of Paul Klee.

The Surrealist painting of Chagall and Chirico and those artists associated with them after the first world war (Jean Lurçat, Joan Miro, Francis Picabia, Pierre Roy and later Picasso) was still formally conceived in accordance with the principles of Cubist and Fauve painting of the day, from which it differed only in the introduction of strange and disturbing subject matter (e.g. Picasso's "Femmes Effrayées au Bord de la Mer" 1923).

The Surrealists at this stage were unorganized, but another trend, led by the writer André Breton, mainly literary in character and largely *Dada* (q.v.) inspired, culminated in the Manifesto of 1924 which denoted the formation of the Surrealist Movement. This new aspect of Surrealism has been renamed *Neo-Surrealism* by certain authorities in order to distinguish betwen the two trends, but as, in fact, the works of the earlier group have been 'adopted' by the latter, the term Surrealism has continued in general use. A new spirit did, however, pervade the now 'official' movement. Painting, as such, was now no longer one of aesthetic concern, but served primarily for the illustration of Surrealist themes which were now based to a large extent on Freudian psychology and included the recording of pseudopsychopathic phenomena as suitable subject matter (Paranoic Criticism). This attitude, however, did not prevent the creation of works of genuine artistic merit as e.g. those of Max Ernst, Hans Arp and André Masson. Use was also made of *Collage* and *Frottage* (qq.v.) and a form of Surrealist sculpture was created (Alberto Giacometti) in addition to the production of Dadaist 'objects' etc.

Surrealism is still practised by such artists as Salvador Dali, Rène Magritte and Yves Tanguy, all of whose work is characterised by a flawless technique in the rendering of intricate detail with a high degree of verisimilitude. The main importance of the movement to-day is the influence it has had, with Cubism and Abstractionism, on the whole field of contemporary art. Being from the first a purely literary form of art, it has, through the work of Paul Nash, particularly influenced the work of the British Neo-Romantic School. See NEO-ROMANTICISM.

Symbolism   In art, symbolism is the expression of an abstract idea in terms of line and colour, or the representation of an object by means of a simple formal equivalent. Symbolism is a feature of much primitive art and is found in the formalism of Byzantine painting, and in some forms of modern Expressionism (Paul Klee, Wassily Kandinsky). In its Freudian sense, symbolism is largely the basis of Surrealism.

Symbolist Movement, The   In 1889 the French painters Emile Bernard and Sérusier formed the Symbolist Movement in revolt against the Impressionist and Realist schools of painting. In so doing they adopted the ideas of Paul Gauguin, with whom they were at the time associated, who had used the title *Synthetic-Symbolism* to describe his paintings of the years 1886-87, his Brittany pictures, e.g. "Jacob Wrestling with the Angel". These were symbolic in subject matter as was also his use of non-imitative line and colour — a procedure which he referred to as ' Synthetic '. Although Gauguin disassociated himself from the group and was displeased at this appropriation of his title, the Symbolist Movement continued to paint and exhibit as such, and were in close association with the *Nabis* and *Rose-Croix* movements (qq.v.). They were inspired, not only by Gauguin, but also by Puvis de Chavannes, and eventually developed a fashion for pastel colours and poetic atmosphere which paralleled the English *Aesthetic Movement* (q.v.).

Symmetry   A disposition of equal elements of a composition about a central axis, producing a sense of repose. (Cf. ASYMMETRY).

Synchromism   A movement in modern painting founded by two American artists, S. Macdonald-Wright and Morgan Russell, in Paris during the early part of the 20th cent. Synchromism is based on the principle that every colour either approaches or recedes from the eye in varying degrees — blue recedes, yellow approaches the eye — and that it is possible to construct a complete scale of colours on this basis. The Synchromists asserted that to paint, for merely realistic purposes, a receding form in a colour that approaches the eye shows a neglect of the structural possibilities of colour, and suggested that a 'pure' kind of painting should be developed in accordance with these principles, using colour composition without drawing. The first works of the Synchromists were intensely-coloured still-lifes and greatly distorted figure paintings painted in bands of pure colour. But several years later they turned to abstract composition in which they attempted to develop colour for purely formal purposes. By 1924, however, they had reverted to a modified use of natural forms.

Synthetic Symbolism   See SYMBOLIST MOVEMENT, THE.

T

Tactile Values   Those qualities in a painting which produce a sense of tangibility in the objects represented.

This phrase appears to have been first used by Mr. Bernard Berenson as a synonym for *form* (q.v.) and he defines it as follows: "Tactile values occur in representations of solid objects when communicated, not as mere reproductions (no matter how veracious), but in a way that stirs the imagination to feel their bulk, heft their weight, realise their potential resistance, span their distance from us, and encourage us, always imaginatively, to come into close touch with, to grasp, to embrace or to walk around them".

Mr. Hilaire Hiler, however, in his *Notes on the Technique of Painting* uses the phrase in another sense as the engendering by the texture of the surface of a painting of ideas associated with the sense of touch, roughness, smoothness, softness etc.

T'ang Art   The golden age of Chinese art was reached in the T'ang Dynasty (618 - 907 A.D.). During those centuries art was largely inspired by Buddhism and expressed itself in painting and sculpture of which there is very little extant, due to its destruction during a reaction in favour of Confucianism which took place during the later years of the dynasty.   Our knowledge of the art of this period is largely gained from writings and from certain examples of Japanese art known to have been inspired by T'ang art which is enough to give us a clear conception of its nature.   Although T'ang art was more naturalistic than the art of preceding dynasties, it was mainly formal and dignified in conception.

In the field of ceramics, there are sufficient specimens reclaimed from burial places to show that the potter had by this time gained the mastery of the medium for which the Chinese have been so justly famed. T'ang ware is simple and graceful in shape and ornament, and the well-known animal figures of this dynasty show undeniable vigour and grasp of form. Glazed pottery was not yet in general use, but both glazed and unglazed ware were produced at the same time during the period.

Tapestry Weaving which permits the production of complex and multi-coloured designs. The warps are placed either horizontally, when it is known as 'low-warp tapestry' or suspended vertically, when it is known as 'high-warp tapestry', and the weft is worked with bobbins, one for each colour used, in a manner which permits the use of an unlimited range of colours. Over 14,000 tints are claimed to have been used in a hanging produced by the famous Gobelins Factory in France.

The art was known to the Egyptians, Babylonians, Greeks and Romans, and reference is made to tapestry in the earliest records of European History. During the Middle Ages tapestry was used extensively for Church decoration, and after the Crusades, tapestry began to be used for domestic decoration after the oriental fashion. The famous Flemish and French tapestries began to be made in the 14th cent., those made at Arras became world famous, and in 1666 Louis XIV established the celebrated Hôtel Royale des Gobelins which has persisted to this day.

Tapestry as an art form is now almost obsolete. In 1933 Madame Cuttoli began a revival of the art and attempted to adapt the work of modern artists to tapestry. Picasso, Rouault, Dufy and Lurçat among others have made designs for tapestries, and examples of the work of these artists in this medium were displayed at the Exhibition of French Tapestries in London in 1947.

Tatlinism The Russian forerunner of *Constructivism* (q.v.) established by Vladimir Tatlin in 1916.

Tatlinism renounced easel pictures and sought to create a new language in art based on the machine, and for this purpose used a wide variety of materials such as wire, wood, nails, string and glass. See COUNTER RELIEF.

Technique The method of executing a work of art as distinct from the expressive element in its composition, from which however, it cannot wholly be separated. Mastery of technique is a valuable asset to an original artist, but cannot compensate for a lack of originality. Much valuable original art has been executed by artists without adequate technique, while much meretricious work is produced by many technically accomplished artists. It is difficult to say how much technique adds to the expressive ability of an original artist, and it might be suggested that a highly developed technique is occasionally a liability. Undoubtedly a great deal of the success of a painter such as the Douanier Rousseau can be attributed to a lack of art school training.

Tectonic Appertaining to building or construction in architecture or kindred arts. The word is used in art criticism to describe the formal or structural qualities in a work of art. See ARCHITECTONIC.

Telamon A male figure used like a *caryatid* (q.v.) as a supporting column.

Tempera This Italian term originally referred to any fluid medium with which pigments could be mixed, including even oil, but it is now used to describe any method by which oil in emulsion (such as linseed oil and glue-water) may be used with water as a diluent. The expression is, however, most usually associated with the particular method of painting with pigments ground with yolk of egg, the traditional method of the early Italian painters. The medium imposes a strict discipline on the artist, as it is quick-drying and does not permit re-touching. Its beauty

136

lies in the quality of its surface which is as hard as enamel, for which reason also it is the most permanent of all painting media.

Tenebrists (painters of darkness)   International group of painters of the early 17th cent. who, inspired by the style of Caravaggio and the *Chiaroscurists* (q.v.), developed a style of painting which emphasised violent contrasts of light and shade usually derived from gloomy interior scenes. By a vulgarised treatment of subject matter they directly opposed the prevailing realism of the Bolognese academic painters.

Tenebrosi   Another name for the *Chiaroscurists* (q.v.).

Ten O'Clock   The title of a highly original and provocative lecture delivered by James McNeill Whistler at ten o'clock on February 20th, 1885, to an audience of "friends and enemies" in which Whistler, among other things, insisted upon the artist's absolute independence. The lecture was repeated in March at Oxford and in April at Cambridge.

Terra-Cotta (It. baked earth)   A fine quality unglazed pottery used since ancient times for statuary, vases and tiles of a characteristic brownish red.

Tesserae   The small cubes of glass, marble, etc. used in mosaic.

Texture   In painting texture refers (1) to the physical characteristics (apart from colour) and minute structure of any surface, such as skin, fabric etc. which the artist is attempting to represent. (2) The characteristics of pigment as handled by the artist (impasto, scumble, glaze etc.) which endow the surface of a picture with distinctive qualities. The procedure is extended by certain advanced schools of painting (Constructivists, Cubists, Surrealists etc.) to include the actual use of materials of varying textures such as newspaper, cork, textiles, and even metal.

Three-Quarter Length   A standard size of canvas (25″ × 30″). Describes also a portrait which extends downwards as far as the hips.

Throwing (Cer.)   In pottery, the act of shaping a vessel on the potter's wheel.

Tonalism   A name given to a number of experiments made by American painters of the late 19th and early 20th cents. in order to paint sunlight. Artists included in the group were George Innes (1825-1894), William Keith (1839-1911) and Henry W. Ranger (1858 - 1916). Various methods were used, a typical example being that of Innes who painted in transparent coats of paint over an initial dry coat of white. The Group was originally inspired by the *Barbizon School* (q.v.) and their experiments were followed by those of the *Luminists* (q.v.).

Tondo   A circular painting or sculptured relief.

Tone   Every colour has its tonal value, that is to say, its strength expressed in terms of lightness or darkness. The best example of tonal values is the translation of colour into monochrome which occurs in photography, whereby objects are no longer related in terms of colour against colour, but in terms of greys ranging from black to white.

Tonk, To   A slang expression used in English studios to describe the process of pressing tissue paper over a wet canvas at the end of the day's work so that when it is removed only a thin film of pigment remains. The purpose is to produce a hazy quality in the finished picture, and the process was habitually used by Professor Henry Tonks from whom the word derives.

Topographical Art   A form of representational art devoted to the description of localities and which therefore comes under the heading of *descriptive art* (q.v.). Topography is a distinctive feature of much English painting, and it is to the topographical drawings of Paul Sandby (1725 - 1809) and Thomas Girtin (1775 - 1802) that the beginnings of English watercolour painting may be attributed. The tradition of topographical painting in England is maintained to-day by John Piper.

Toreutics   The art of embossing, carving in relief and chasing with special reference to metals.

Tortillon   A small variety of *stump* (q.v.).

Totalitarian Art   Certain authoritarian governments have encouraged the production of painting and sculpture with the slogan "Art for the State's Sake", and discouraged the individualistic work of original artists.   The art so produced, which includes the officially imposed architecture, was based on superficially classical themes, easily assimilable by the masses, and mainly concerned with the propagation of totalitarian ideologies.   Painting and sculpture were devoted to "heroic" portraits of the leaders and public figures and symbolic glorifications of the state-approved 'types' of the Worker, the Soldier and the Mother.   Architecture served to impress and overawe with huge buildings in the Neo-Classic manner symbolic of the power and importance of the State.   This kind of art is best exemplified by the Novecento and Soviet Realism movements in Italy and Russia, and in the Neo-Classical art of the Third Reich.

Tournai School   A Flemish school of popular religious art that originated at Tournai in the 15th cent.   The leaders were Rogier Van der Weyden and Robert Campion. The school strongly influenced contemporary painting at Haarlem, Ghent and Louvaine.

Tours, School of   A Carolingian school of illuminators and miniature painters in the early part of the 9th cent.

Tracery   The ornamental carving of windows and panelling etc. which is the distinctive feature in Gothic architecture. Plate tracery is the earliest form where the stone is pierced by the decoration. Bar tracery is later and built up of segments of carved stone.

Transitional Style   This term may be used to describe the period of change from one Gothic style of architecture to another which usually took place in the last quarter of the century. The expression is more precisely used, however, to describe the change from Norman to Early English.

Trecento (It. three hundred)   Used to describe 14th cent. Italian painting.

Triptych   An altarpiece in the form of three hinged panels bearing paintings generally designed as a single composition.

Tromphe L'Oeil   A French expression (literally cheat-the-eye) used to describe representational painting where the intention of the artist is to achieve a high degree of verisimilitude. Ideally, such painting would deceive the spectator into accepting it as the actual object depicted, and the history of art abounds in anecdotes in which this is said to have taken place. This type of art has been long held in popular esteem, but in fact it is a mediocre accomplishment requiring only a high degree of technical ability. The meretricious attraction of trompe l'oeil soon palls unless accompanied by some genuine artistic merit which accounts for the worthlessness of much work of the late 19th cent. painters. The device is extensively used by modern commercial artists, and is also exploited by Surrealist painters.

Tuscan School   An alternative name for *The Florentine School* (q.v.).

'291' Group   A group of American artists who took their name from the address of the gallery,

291, Fifth Avenue, New York, where they met. The group was led by the owner of the gallery, Alfred Steiglitz, who organized from 1908 to 1917, a series of exhibitions of Post-Impressionist art, etchings, prints, photographs and paintings. These exhibitions introduced the work of important European painters to America almost for the first time and in addition collective exhibitions and one-man shows of such advanced American painters as Dove, Marin, Maurer, Hartley and Weber were held.

U

Umbrian School   The 15th cent. Italian school of Umbria is most notable for producing the genius of Raphael (1483-1520), Perugino (1446-1523), Piero della Francesca (1420?-1492) and Luca Signorelli (1441-1523). The work of this school is renowned for the development of space effects and landscape painting and is characterised by a distinctly suave quality. The school was a major influence in the art of Renaissance Italy.

Uncial   Word used to describe a form of writing, common in early Greek and Latin manuscripts, in which each letter is formed separately in a loose rounded style. Also sometimes applied to capital letters of large size.

Under Glaze Painting (Cer.)   Decoration applied directly to the biscuit of porcelain before covering with transparent glaze.

Unit One   This group of English painters, sculptors and architects was formed early in 1933 by a number of already established artists, who, while remaining intensely individualistic in their creative work, felt themselves drawn together by a mutual sympathy as representatives of the truly contemporary spirit for which they stood. The group consisted of the painters Paul Nash, Ben Nicholson, Tristram Hillier, Edward Burra, Edward Wadsworth, John Armstrong and John Bigg, the sculptors, Barbara Hepworth and Henry Moore and the architects, Wells Coates and Colin Lucas.

The announcement of the formation of the group was the subject of a letter by Paul Nash printed in *The Times* of June 2nd, 1934, the text of which is reprinted together with details of the organisation in the publication *Unit One*, edited by Herbert Read and published by Cassell in 1934.

Universals   In abstract art the expression 'universal' refers to the underlying significant structure of an object as opposed to the 'accidentals' of its accepted visual appearance.

Unschooled Painters   There have been painters whose technical ability does not betray their lack of orthodox art school training, and who have taken their place with ease among their trained associates. The term 'unschooled', however, is more usually applied to those painters whose want of technique gives their work a naive, almost gauche, quality, but whose originality of vision is stated with frankness and sincerity.   Such painters, often styled 'primitives' are the French Douanier Rousseau, Vivin, Bombois and Bauchant, the English Alfred Wallis and the American 'Grandma' Moses.

V

Values   The relationship of two or more tones is known as *value*. The accurate rendering of values is more important than colour in the expression of natural appearances.   See TONE.

Varnish   A substance of resinous origin, sometimes used as a dryer in oil painting, but most often used as a protective film applied over the surface of a finished painting. Owing to the fact that it dries faster than oil, it must be applied some considerable time, six months or more, after the completion of the picture in order to avoid cracking. Varnish becomes discoloured after a long period, which largely accounts for the dull tones of 'Old Masters', a fact which has been amply demonstrated by the cleaning of the pictures in the National Gallery. Many painters of the 19th cent, simulated the 'antique' effect by applying a toned varnish.

Vehicle   In painting, the substance (such as oil, gum, glue, etc.) with which pigments are bound or tempered and in which they are ground.

Velatura (It.)   A method of glazing used by early Italian painters. The colour is rubbed on by all the fingers or the flat of the hand. The object was to cover the picture with thin, even colour and to avoid the interstices left by the brush.

Venetian School   During that period of Italian art known as the High Renaissance, Venice was second only to Florence in pre-eminence in the arts; and as the century progressed, and the prosperity of her merchant princes increased, Venice assumed full leadership. a position which she maintained until Italy ceased to be the artistic centre of Europe.

Unlike the Florentine artists, whose approach to painting was so largely intellectual, the Venetians were primarily concerned with the world of the senses, and it is perhaps for this reason that their outstanding achievement lay in their instinctive use of direct colour for its own sake and not as an adjunct to design. This attitude no doubt resulted from their almost exclusive use of oil paint instead of tempera, and the technique which they were therefore able to develop in the use of transparent glazes.

Merchants and princes rather than the Church were their patrons, and their art was therefore more secular than religious. Even where religious themes were used, the subject was portrayed in Venetian dress and setting. Landscape in their hands became an integral part of the picture instead of the merely conventional background as with the Florentines.

The great masters of the school were Bellini (1426-1507), his pupil Giorgione (1478-1510), Titian (1477-1576) and his pupil Tintoretto (1518-1594) and Veronese (1528 - 1588).

Verisimiltude The accurate representation of mechanical vision in painting, and the basis of *naturalism* in art in which, however, the artist invariably adds a certain degree of feeling which is the expression of his emotional reaction to the subject depicted. The term verisimiltude is roughly the equivalent of the French *trompe l'oeil* (q.v.).

Vernissage (Fr. varnishing) Refers to a preliminary gathering at an exhibition of art before the official opening, at which the artists frequently varnished their pictures.

Vignette A small illustration or ornament, used principally in book production at the beginnings and ends of chapters, the design being made to fade off into the paper.

Volume By his handling of volumes, an artist is able to express his feeling for three-dimensional form in addition to that which he has for pattern and surface design.

In painting, volume is expressed mainly by the painter's use of light and shade, although certain subtle uses of colour to define or soften edges will impart a sense of solidity, while in draughtsmanship the artist will rely mainly on the ability of his line to depict contours and suggest the volumes which they contain.

The subject is of primary importance to the sculptor, who is, of course, concerned with the relationships of actual volumes with each other and the space they occupy, rather than with their representation in an imaginary setting.

Vorticism   The *Vorticist Movement* was founded by the English artist, Wyndham Lewis, in 1914 at the same time as the publication of the first issue of *Blast*, a Vorticist manifesto. Vorticism was based on Cubist and Futurist theories with a leaning towards the literary and social doctrines of the latter. The founder was himself probably the most successful exponent of the theory in a group which included Edward Wadsworth and William Roberts.

W

Wanderers, The   A late 19th cent. movement in Russian art led by Nicholas Kramskoy while still a student at the Imperial Academy, in revolt against academic dogma. In common with the general revolutionary tendencies of the time, it aimed to carry art to the people and for this reason was strictly realistic and didactic, being less concerned with aesthetics than with moral and social problems.

Wash   In water colour painting and drawing, a thin application of transparent colour.

Water Colour Painting   Any method of painting which uses water as a medium or diluent is properly speaking a water colour method (*gouache* or *distemper* (qq.v.)) but the term is more usually applied to the art of painting in which the pigment is bound with gums of various kinds and diluted with water. The most characteristic use of the medium is that common in this country (and in fact known abroad as the English Method) which applies the colour in transparent washes using the white of the paper for high lights and eschewing the use of white pigment. The French method, on the other hand, makes use of opaque white with which to mix the lighter tones and uses washes for the darker passages. This method is also known as *Body-colour*.

Wax Painting   A rarely-used method of painting in which pigments are mixed with molten beeswax. The method is sometimes used with ordinary oil pigments from which the greater part of the oil has been absorbed by blotting paper; the great advantage being its permanence when used in *impasto*. The apparently frenzied brushwork of Van Gogh, for example, is actually built up of oil and wax impasto. See also ENCAUSTIC.

Wood Engraving and Woodcuts   Both these methods of making prints from wood blocks are similar in that they are printed by the relief process (i.e. the part of the design to be printed is left raised on the block), but they differ in the technique employed and the characteristic finish. Wood engraving is executed by various kinds of gravers on the very close end-grain of boxwood, while woodcuts are done on the side-grain of a softer wood, such as pear, with a knife. The nature of the tool used in wood engraving is reflected by the fluid, graphic line, while a tonal quality is achieved by hatching and stippling in close white lines and dots. The knife, on the other hand, dictates a certain angularity to the line in a woodcut.

Woodcuts were employed from very early times for the illustration of books until replaced by steel engraving, and line engraving was used until the close of the 19th cent. for newspaper and magazine work, the artists achieving a high degree of skill in imitating paintings and photographs, a skill, however, which abused the natural characteristics of the medium. The invention of the photographic block, however, displaced line engraving and the method fell into disuse until revived by modern artists who concerned themselves with restoring its original charm.

Japanese prints inspired the revival of the modern woodcut, and present day use of this medium is based on Japanese methods, using several colours in one print. Each colour necessitates the use of a separate block, and frequently, instead of printing a large area in a flat colour, the artist uses his brush when applying the ink to achieve a toned effect, sometimes even manipulating the wet colour after printing.

World of Art Group   A group of Russian painters, led by Benois, which came into being as a protest against the tenets of *The Wanderers* (q.v.). The Group held that the interpretation of nature was of greater importance than its imitation and built its creed round the slogan 'Art for Art's Sake'. Decorative art was perhaps its most important aspect and its greatest influence was felt in the theatre (Leon Bakst), mural painting and book illustration.

X

X Group   An association of English Post Impressionist painters founded in 1920 which was largely the post-war continuation of the *Vorticist Movement* (q.v.). In addition to the original Vorticist artists (Wyndham Lewis, Wadsworth and Roberts) the group included certain of the more progressive members of the London Group: Charles Ginner, Frank Dobson, H. McKnight Kauffer, Frederick Etchells.

Xoanon   An early archaic Greek statue, carved in wood for religious purposes. There are no longer any examples in existence and our knowledge of them is obtained from Classical literature.

X-Ray Drawings   A form of naturalistic art practised by Melanesian natives and aboriginees of the northern territories of Australia, in which the artist represents inner parts of human beings and animals (spine, ribs etc.) because he knows they exist and have a particular interest for him.

Xylography   The art of engraving on wood.

Y

Yuan Art   The art of the Mongol Dynasty established in China during the years 1280 A.D. to 1368 A.D. may be regarded for all practical purposes as an extension of the Sung period, but is distinguished by the vast number of hunting pictures reflecting the tastes of the new rulers.

Z

Zoomorphic   The representation of animal forms in decorative art, and ZOOMORPH, the animal so represented.

Zophorus (Lat. 'animal bearing')   In ancient archaeology the representation of men and animals in relief on a frieze.